Learning VMware NSX

Virtualize your network with this step-by-step configuration guide to installing, configuring, and managing VMware NSX

Ranjit Singh Thakurratan

[PACKT] enterprise
PUBLISHING
professional expertise distilled

BIRMINGHAM - MUMBAI

Learning VMware NSX

First published: January 2016

Production reference: 1220116

Published by Packt Publishing Ltd.
Livery Place
35 Livery Street
Birmingham B3 2PB, UK.

ISBN 978-1-78588-688-1

www.packtpub.com

Credits

Author
Ranjit Singh Thakurratan

Reviewers
Jonathan Frappier

Anthony Spiteri

Commissioning Editor
Veena Pagare

Acquisition Editor
Meeta Rajani

Content Development Editor
Priyanka Mehta

Technical Editor
Menza Mathew

Copy Editor
Kausambhi Majumdar

Project Coordinator
Izzat Contractor

Proofreader
Safis Editing

Indexer
Tejal Daruwale Soni

Production Coordinator
Aparna Bhagat

Cover Work
Aparna Bhagat

About the Author

Ranjit Singh Thakurratan (RJ) is a VMware vExpert (2014 and 2015) and works as a VMware cloud solutions architect, specializing in architecting Enterprise cloud solutions. He works for Rackspace—the #1 managed cloud company and home of Fanatical Support—which is based out of San Antonio, Texas.

RJ holds a master's degree in information technology—infrastructure assurance, an engineering degree in computer science, and has over ten years of hands-on IT experience. He has presented at numerous VMUG UserCon conferences held at Boston, Washington DC, New York, Denver, and Dallas. He also runs a technology blog, www.rjapproves.com, and can be reached via his Twitter handle—@RJAPPROVES. Apart from technology, RJ is also interested in astrophysics, animal welfare, and open source projects.

One of his favorite quotes is:

> *"The greatness of a nation and its moral progress can be judged by the way its animals are treated."*

> *–Mahatma Gandhi*

I would like to thank my parents, Jagat Singh and Thakur Sindhu Kumari, for making me the man I am today, and my brother, Manjit Singh, for being supportive all along. Lastly, to my lovely dog, Shyla Singh, who loves selflessly and has kept me on the move.

About the Reviewers

Jonathan Frappier is a technology professional focused on working with organizations to understand business operations and requirements and then design, transform, and support technology solutions and teams that leverage modern trends in virtualization, cloud computing, DevOps, and social enterprise collaboration.

He works on a wide range of technology, from firewalls and switches to Windows, Active Directory, Exchange, VMware vSphere, storage, backups, disaster recovery, and support custom-developed software, in both large and small companies where technology is heavily relied upon.

> I would like to thank my parents and grandparents, my wife and daughter, and the amazing virtualization community for everything you do every day—without you, opportunities like this would not exist.

Anthony Spiteri has been working as a hosting and cloud professional since 2002, and in that time, he has been privileged to work at some of the leading service providers in Australia. Anthony has developed a true passion for his work and has worked on products and services that deliver high quality results through leading edge technologies. As a lead architect at ZettaGrid, he has helped push the boundaries of virtualization and cloud by leading product development and looking into doing great things with a great technology.

As a VMware vExpert and vChampion, Anthony has been able to build on his community work by delivering talks and presentations at various events locally and overseas. He runs the Virtualization is Life! blog at `http://anthonyspiteri.net`, and he is a contributor to Planet V12n, OneCloud Road, and AussievMafia. He has gained high levels of technical praise for his posts and comments on all things hosting- and cloud-related.

www.PacktPub.com

Support files, eBooks, discount offers, and more

For support files and downloads related to your book, please visit www.PacktPub.com.

Did you know that Packt offers eBook versions of every book published, with PDF and ePub files available? You can upgrade to the eBook version at www.PacktPub.com and as a print book customer, you are entitled to a discount on the eBook copy. Get in touch with us at service@packtpub.com for more details.

At www.PacktPub.com, you can also read a collection of free technical articles, sign up for a range of free newsletters and receive exclusive discounts and offers on Packt books and eBooks.

https://www2.packtpub.com/books/subscription/packtlib

Do you need instant solutions to your IT questions? PacktLib is Packt's online digital book library. Here, you can search, access, and read Packt's entire library of books.

Why subscribe?

- Fully searchable across every book published by Packt
- Copy and paste, print, and bookmark content
- On demand and accessible via a web browser

Free access for Packt account holders

If you have an account with Packt at www.PacktPub.com, you can use this to access PacktLib today and view 9 entirely free books. Simply use your login credentials for immediate access.

Instant updates on new Packt books

Get notified! Find out when new books are published by following @PacktEnterprise on Twitter or the *Packt Enterprise* Facebook page.

Table of Contents

Preface

Networking is the most critical component of any IT architecture. Architects always want to lay the right foundations of networks and solve networking issues before the computation and storage is looked at. This is why I have always felt the need to have a better understanding of networking and how things work.

Network virtualization technology allowed me to have a behind-the-scenes, hands-on look at how networking works and the concepts that made it happen. The ability to deploy virtual appliances such as switches, load balancers, and routers and examine their functionality was very appealing. The pace at which I learned network virtualization (NSX) gave me the confidence to grow in a field in which I thought I lacked significant knowledge. Through my journey, I understood that network virtualization not only made me think like a network engineer, but also made me apply networking concepts very creatively to a virtualized environment, and this made it all the more appealing. What was complex before, now became extremely simple.

In 2015, I went about giving presentations at multiple VMUG UserCon sessions all around the country. My presentation was on *Getting started with VMware NSX - Basics and Best Practices*. Here, my aim was not to talk about what NSX can do but to talk about how easy it was to get started with NSX and also to squash some common misconceptions about it. I wasn't sure whether this was a topic worth talking about and wasn't expecting a large crowd. (My time slot to present was right after lunch, which wasn't very encouraging.)

Soon, I was proved wrong. In each and every city where I gave my presentations, all of my sessions had a full audience. People were eager to know how to get started with NSX and in fact, preferred this presentation to any of the other VMware NSX presentations happening at the same conference. I was able to quickly identify the huge knowledge gap and the plethora of common misconceptions about NSX and network virtualization, in general. I also observed that many of the attendees were network administrators with an interest in network virtualization.

This feedback from the tech community gave me a desire to write a book that covers the basics and teaches how to get started with NSX. I want to connect to the day-to-day administrator and the network engineer who is wondering how all the dots connect, and this is something I am passionate about. The book explains the basics and covers the deployment of the various features of network virtualization in simple and clear language and with screenshots that allow you to visualize the workflow as you read. I did have to work around a page restriction set by the publisher, so I focused on the most commonly used or sought-after features in the book even though I covered all of the NSX features and functionality. The audience feedback from various conferences helped me greatly.

I hope you enjoy working with this book and that it helps you to learn to use and understand NSX and network virtualization.

What this book covers

Chapter 1, An Introduction to Network Virtualization, gets you started with an introduction to network virtualization and an overview of its concepts. You will briefly learn about some of NSX's features and capabilities. We also have a NSX limits table to help you understand NSX's capabilities.

Chapter 2, NSX Core Components, talks about all the different components of NSX and how they all work together. You will also learn about VXLAN architecture that is the backbone of overlay or virtual networking. We will also briefly talk about transport zones that define the scope of a virtual network. You will learn about NSX Edge services and the distributed firewall as well.

Chapter 3, NSX Installation and Configuration, is where we will start deploying and configuring NSX. We will go over the installation process step by step and then configure our NSX deployment with a vCenter server. You will learn how to manage NSX using the vSphere web client and build your control and data planes.

Chapter 4, NSX Functional Services, discusses the deployment and configuration of different NSX services, such as logical switching, L2 bridging, and Edge gateway services. We will go over the configuration of transport zones and logical switching step by step. This will be an interesting chapter, where you will also learn the deployment of Edge appliances and set up L2 bridging, which allows you to extend a layer 2 network into NSX.

Chapter 5, Edge Services Gateway, discusses the NSX Edge gateway, which offers a lot of features and capabilities. We will go deeper into the services offered by the Edge gateway and look at how to deploy and configure them. We will look at how to configure routing and load balancing. You will also spend some time learning to set up DHCP and DNS services.

Chapter 6, Data Security, discusses one of the most important capabilities of NSX, its security, and also discusses the different NSX security offerings. We will discuss and learn how to set up security groups and configure them by mapping a security group to a specific policy. You will also learn briefly about the network extensibility feature of NSX.

Chapter 7, Monitoring, looks at how to enable monitoring for our environment using NSX. Activity monitoring is one of the features of NSX that is a boon for network and system administrators. You will learn how to configure it along with generating a virtual machine activity report. You will also learn about flow monitoring and Traceflow, which can simulate and allow you to test the network.

Chapter 8, Managing NSX, talks about NSX administrative tasks such as backup and restore and NSX Manager settings. We will revisit NSX Manager and explore all the different settings that can be set. We will look at setting up syslog, time, and DNS settings. We will also look at taking controller snapshots as well. We will also have a look at the setup of our NSX Manager with CA signed certificates along with configuring NSX with a domain.

Chapter 9, Conclusion, is the concluding chapter that includes important information and links

What you need for this book

Although you can dive right into this book, I recommend setting up a modest home lab of three servers running VMware's ESXi and vCenter. You are also encouraged to spend some time exploring the **hands on labs** offered for free by VMware. The specific NSX labs that will help you greatly are **HOL-SDC-1603** and **HOL-SDC-1625**. These labs will help you get started with NSX without having to worry about the intricacies of having to set it up.

You can get to "hands on labs" by going to `http://labs.hol.vmware.com` and searching for the two labs I mentioned earlier.

Who this book is for

This book is for those who want to learn how to install, manage, and configure the VMware NSX Network Virtualization platform. If you want to explore, understand, or deploy VMware NSX in your environment, this book is for you. Also, this book can assist you in preparing for VMware NSX certification. Knowledge of the basic networking concepts and VMware components such as vCenter and vSphere is required.

Conventions

In this book, you will find a number of text styles that distinguish between different kinds of information. Here are some examples of these styles and an explanation of their meaning.

Code words in text, database table names, folder names, filenames, file extensions, pathnames, dummy URLs, user input, and Twitter handles are shown as follows: "We can include other contexts through the use of the `include` directive."

A block of code is set as follows:

```
[root@host:~] esxcli software vib list | grepesx
esx-vsip6.0.0-0.0.2732470    VMware  VMwareCertified    2015-05-29
esx-vxlan6.0.0-0.0.2732470   VMware  VMwareCertified    2015-05-29
```

When we wish to draw your attention to a particular part of a code block, the relevant lines or items are set in bold:

```
[root@host:~] esxcli software vib list | grepesx
esx-vsip6.0.0-0.0.2732470    VMware  VMwareCertified    2015-05-29
esx-vxlan6.0.0-0.0.2732470   VMware  VMwareCertified    2015-05-29
```

New terms and **important words** are shown in bold. Words that you see on the screen, for example, in menus or dialog boxes, appear in the text like this: "Click on **Change** in the **Syslog servers** row."

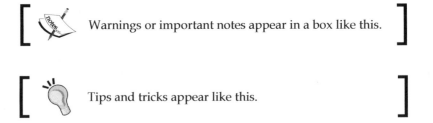

> Warnings or important notes appear in a box like this.

> Tips and tricks appear like this.

Reader feedback

Feedback from our readers is always welcome. Let us know what you think about this book—what you liked or disliked. Reader feedback is important for us as it helps us develop titles that you will really get the most out of.

To send us general feedback, simply e-mail `feedback@packtpub.com`, and mention the book's title in the subject of your message.

If there is a topic that you have expertise in and you are interested in either writing or contributing to a book, see our author guide at `www.packtpub.com/authors`.

Customer support

Now that you are the proud owner of a Packt book, we have a number of things to help you to get the most from your purchase.

Downloading the example code

You can download the example code files from your account at `http://www.packtpub.com` for all the Packt Publishing books you have purchased. If you purchased this book elsewhere, you can visit `http://www.packtpub.com/support` and register to have the files e-mailed directly to you.

Errata

Although we have taken every care to ensure the accuracy of our content, mistakes do happen. If you find a mistake in one of our books—maybe a mistake in the text or the code—we would be grateful if you could report this to us. By doing so, you can save other readers from frustration and help us improve subsequent versions of this book. If you find any errata, please report them by visiting `http://www.packtpub.com/submit-errata`, selecting your book, clicking on the **Errata Submission Form** link, and entering the details of your errata. Once your errata are verified, your submission will be accepted and the errata will be uploaded to our website or added to any list of existing errata under the Errata section of that title.

To view the previously submitted errata, go to `https://www.packtpub.com/books/content/support` and enter the name of the book in the search field. The required information will appear under the **Errata** section.

Piracy

Piracy of copyrighted material on the Internet is an ongoing problem across all media. At Packt, we take the protection of our copyright and licenses very seriously. If you come across any illegal copies of our works in any form on the Internet, please provide us with the location address or website name immediately so that we can pursue a remedy.

Please contact us at copyright@packtpub.com with a link to the suspected pirated material.

We appreciate your help in protecting our authors and our ability to bring you valuable content.

Questions

If you have a problem with any aspect of this book, you can contact us at questions@packtpub.com, and we will do our best to address the problem.

1

An Introduction to Network Virtualization

This chapter begins with a brief introduction to Network Virtualization followed by an overview of its concepts. We then introduce VMware's NSX-V Network Virtualization solution that allows you to deploy and manage your own software-defined networking stack. We will go over all the features and services of NSX followed by its configuration maximums. By the end of this chapter, you will have a thorough understanding of the concepts of Network Virtualization and NSX-V as a Network Virtualization solution.

In this chapter, we will cover the following:

- An introduction to Network Virtualization
- The concepts of Network Virtualization
- An introduction to the NSX-V Network virtualization platform
- NSX features and services
- NSX configuration maximums

An introduction to Network Virtualization

Today's datacenter demands have undergone a paradigm shift from what they were a decade ago. As the cloud consumption model is being rapidly adopted across the industry, the need for on-demand provisioning of compute, storage, and networking resources is greater than ever. One of the biggest contributing factors to enable the cloud consumption model is **Server virtualization**. Server virtualization has enabled fast consumption of compute resources along with add-on functionality and services. Snapshots, clones, and templates are all now easier than ever with Server virtualization.

If you have worked in a datacenter, you would agree that networking is always challenging to work with. Once the networking design is established, any changes that need to be made are always challenging because of a lack of flexibility due to increasing complexity and demands on the environment. While compute and storage have rapidly improved on their speed of deployment and consumption, networking continues to remain a challenge in today's environments where simple tasks, such as creating a new VLAN, are becoming increasingly complex and time-consuming.

 A metaphor: Today's networking is similar to building roads and highways in a city. Once you have the highways and roads established, it is not easy to expand them or simply remove and replace them without affecting the city or the traffic. You always have to think forward and have to build to handle future growth and have the flexibility to expand and maintain. Similarly, traditional networks in a datacenter have to be built to handle future growth and should be flexible enough to allow for changes as they happen.

Network Virtualization is the "virtualization" of network resources using software and networking hardware to enable faster provisioning and deployment of networking resources. Network Virtualization lays the foundation for Software Defined Networking that allows instant deployment of services to be offered to the consumers. Services such as Edge Gateways, VPN, DHCP, DNS, and load balancers can be instantly provisioned and deployed because of the software aspect of Network Virtualization. The networking hardware allows physical connectivity, while the software is where all the network logic resides that allows a feature-rich network service offering.

Network Virtualization allows the consumption of simplified logical networking devices and services that are completely abstracted from the complexities of the underlying physical network. Lastly, Network Virtualization is the key for a Software-Defined Datacenter (SDDC).

The concepts of Network Virtualization

Now that we have defined what network virtualization is about, let's go over some of the key concepts of network virtualization and software defined networking:

- **Decoupling**: An important concept of Network Virtualization is the decoupling of software and the networking hardware. The software works independently of the networking hardware that physically interconnects the infrastructure. Remember that your throughput on the wire will be always limited by your network hardware performance.

- **Control Plane**: The decoupling of software and networking hardware allows you to control your network better because all the logic resides in software. This control aspect of your network is called the control plane. The control plane provides the means to configure, monitor, and troubleshoot and also allows automation against the network.

- **Data Plane**: The networking hardware forms the data plane where all the data is forwarded from source to destination. The management of data resides in the control plane; however, the data plane consists of all the networking hardware whose primary function is to forward traffic over the wire from source to destination. The data plane holds all the forwarding tables that are constantly updated by the control plane. This also prevents any traffic interruptions if there is a loss of the control plane because the networking hardware, which constitutes the data plane, will continue to function without interruptions.

- **API**: Application Programming Interface or API is one of the important aspects of a virtualized Network that allows us to have true software-defined networking by instantly changing the network behavior. With the API, you can now instantly deploy rich network services in your existing network. Network services such as Edge Gateway, VPN, firewalls, and load balancers can all be deployed on the fly by means of an API.

An introduction to the NSX-V network virtualization platform

VMware NSX-V is a network virtualization platform that allows us to have software-defined networks and is a critical component of software-defined datacenter architecture. VMware's NSX-V software abstracts the underlying physical network by introducing a software layer that makes it easy to consume network resources by creating multiple virtual networks. NSX-V also allows the deployment of multiple logical network services on top of the abstracted layer.

 VMware acquired NSX from Nicira in July, 2012. Nicira's NSX was primarily being used for network virtualization in a Xen-based hypervisor.

VMware now has two flavors of NSX: NSX-V and NSX-MH. NSX-V is NSX for VMware-based hypervisor, while NSX-Multi Hypervisor (NSX-MH) is for OpenStack environments. The two versions have many similarities but are also dissimilar in some aspects. This book covers only the NSX-VMware (NSX-V) version of NSX. NSX-V will be referred to as NSX in the rest of the book.

The following figure represents the software abstraction of the physical network and networking hardware by NSX. This is synonymous with how VMware vSphere hypervisor achieves the software abstraction of CPU, memory, and storage that makes it possible to create multiple virtual machines.

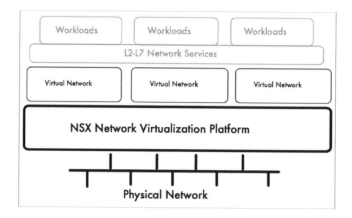

Similar to how the vSphere hypervisor allows you to create, delete, take a snapshot of, and monitor a virtual machine, NSX also allows you to programmatically create, delete, take a snapshot of, and monitor a virtual network. NSX can be deployed on your current physical network infrastructure and does not require you to upgrade your existing infrastructure. Lastly, NSX deployment is not disruptive to your existing network and traffic. It can be seamlessly deployed on top of your existing infrastructure, and the consumption of its services can take place in conjunction with your traditional network.

NSX features and services

Before we get started with NSX, it is important to understand some of its features and services. Some NSX features are listed as follows. We will discuss these features in greater detail in the following chapters.

NSX 6.2 is the current NSX version as of this writing.

- **Logical switching**: NSX allows the ability to create L2 and L3 logical switching that allows workload isolation and the separation of IP address space between logical networks. NSX can create logical broadcast domains in the virtual space that prevent the need to create any logical networks on physical switches. This means you can are no longer limited to 4096 physical broadcast domains (VLANs).

- **NSX Gateway Services**: The Edge Gateway services interconnect your logical networks with your physical networks. This means a virtual machine connected to a logical network can send and receive traffic directly to your physical network through the gateway.

- **Logical Routing**: Multiple virtual broadcast domains (logical networks) can be created using NSX. As multiple virtual machines subscribe to these domains, it becomes important to be able to route traffic from one logical switch to another. Logical routing helps to achieve this by routing traffic between logical switches, or even between a logical switch and the public networks. Logical routing can be extended to perform east-west routing that saves unnecessary network hops by increasing network efficiency. Logical routers can also provide north-south connectivity by allowing access to workloads living in physical networks. Logical routers also help to avoid the hairpinning of traffic, thereby increasing network efficiency.

> East-west traffic is the traffic between the virtual machines within a datacenter. In the current context, this typically will be the traffic between logical switches in a VMware environment.
>
> North-south traffic is the traffic moving in and out of your datacenter. This is any traffic that either enters your datacenter or leaves your datacenter.

- **Logical firewall**: NSX allows you to have the options of a Distributed Logical Firewall and an Edge firewall for use within your software-defined networking architecture. A distributed logical firewall allows you to build rules based on attributes that include not just IP addresses and VLANs, but also virtual machine names and vCenter objects. The Edge Gateway features a firewall service that can be used to impose security and access restrictions on north-south traffic.

- **Extensibility**: NSX allows you to integrate with many third-party partner solutions. There are many VMware partners who offer solutions such as traffic monitoring, IDS, and application firewall services that can integrate directly into NSX. This enhances management and end user experience by having one management system to work with.

The features listed previously enable NSX to offer a wide variety of services that can be applied to your infrastructure. These services can be deployed and configured by the NSX API as well. Some of the NSX services are listed as follows:

- **Load balancer** NSX Edge offers a variety of services, and logical load balancer is one of them. The logical load balancer distributes incoming requests among multiple servers to allow load distribution while abstracting this functionality from end users. The logical load balancer can also be used as a **high availability (HA)** mechanism to ensure that your application has the most uptime.

- **Virtual Private Networks (VPN)**: The Edge offers a VPN service that allows you to provision a secure encrypted connectivity for end users to your applications and workloads. The Edge VPN service offers SSL-VPN plus that allows user access and IPSEC site-to-site connectivity that allows two sites to be interconnected securely.

- **Dynamic Host Configuration Protocol (DHCP)**: NSX Edge offers DHCP services that allows IP address pooling and also static IP assignments. An administrator can now rely on the DHCP service to manage all the IP addresses in your environment rather than maintaining a separate DHCP service. The DHCP service can also relay DHCP requests to your existing DHCP server. The NSX Edge DHCP service can relay any DHCP requests generated from your virtual machines to a pre-existing physical or virtual DHCP server without any interruptions.

- **Domain Name System (DNS)**: NSX Edge offers a DNS relay service that can relay any DNS requests to an external DNS server.

- **Service composer**: The service composer allows you to allocate network and multiple security services to security groups. Services are automatically applied to virtual machines that are part of these security groups.

- **Data Security**: NSX Data Security provides visibility to sensitive data, ensures data protection, and reports back on any compliance violations. A data security scan on designated virtual machines allows NSX to analyze and report back on any violations based on the security policy that applies to these virtual machines.

Other NSX features include **cross-vCenter networking** and security, which allows you to manage multiple vCenter NSX environments using a primary NSX manager. This not only permits a centralized management, but also extends one or more services and features across multiple vCenter environments. We will discuss more about cross vCenter networking in the upcoming chapters.

NSX configuration maximums

Let's take a look at what NSX configuration maximums are. VMware has not published an official document, so the limits listed in the following tables were gathered by reviewing the NSX documentation and from online research. Some websites that contributed include www.vmguru.com.

Some of these limits are hard limits, but most are soft limits beyond which VMware does not support such configurations. For example if you exceed the number of concurrent connections per Edge Gateway, it will affect your gateway's performance but won't cause it to halt or reject new connections. The hard limits versus soft limits documentation is not explicitly published; however, VMware NSX support can clarify the differences if needed. Chances are that you will scale out your environment before reaching these maximums.

The following tables are the maximums for NSX.

 Configuration maximums can differ based on software releases. Always refer to the most up-to-date documentation to ensure accuracy.

The following table shows the limits for **NSX – vCenter Maximums**:

Description	Limit
vCenters	1
NSX Managers	1
DRS Clusters	12
NSX Controllers	3
Hosts per cluster	32
Hosts per Transport Zone	256

A **Transport Zone** defines the scope of a logical switch and can span one or more vSphere clusters. We will discuss this in greater detail in the upcoming chapters.

The following table shows the limits for **Switching Maximums**:

Description	Limit
Logical Switches	10,000
Logical Switch Ports	50,000
Bridges per Distributed Logical Router	500

The following table shows the limits for **Distributed Logical Firewall Maximums**:

Description	Limit
Rules per NSX Manager	100,000
Rules per VM	1,000
Rules per Host	10,000
Concurrent connections per Host	2,000,000
Security Groups per NSX Manager	10,000

The following table shows the limits for **Distributed Logical Router (DLR) Maximums**:

Description	Limit
DLRs per Host	1,000
DLR per NSX Manager	1,200
Interfaces per DLR	999
Uplink interfaces per DLR	8
Active routes per DLR	2,000
Active routes per NSX Manager	12,000
OSPF Adjacencies per DLR	10
BGP Peers per DLR	10

 Open Shortest Path First (OSPF) and **Border Gateway Protocol (BGP)** are routing protocols.

The following table shows the limits for **NSX Edge Services Gateway (ESG) Maximums**:

Description	Limit
Total number of Edge Service Gateways per NSX Manager	2,000
Interfaces per ESG (internal, uplink, or trunk)	10
Sub-interfaces on a trunk	200
NAT Rules per ESG	2,000
Static routes per ESG	2,048

The following table shows the limits for **Edge Services Gateway Compact Maximums**:

Description	Limit
OSPF Routes per ESG	20,000
OSPF Adjacencies per ESG	10
BGP Peers per ESG	10
BGP Routes per ESG	20,000
Total Routes per ESG	20,000
Concurrent connections per ESG	64,000

The following table shows the limits for **Edge Services Gateway Large Maximums**:

Description	Limit
OSPF Routes per ESG	50,000
OSPF Adjacencies per ESG	20
BGP Peers per ESG	20
BGP Routes per ESG	50,000
Total Routes per ESG	50,000
Concurrent connections per ESG	1,000,000

The following table shows the limits for **Edge Services Gateway X-Large Maximums**:

Description	Limit
OSPF Routes per ESG	100,000
OSPF Adjacencies per ESG	40
BGP Peers per ESG	50
BGP Routes per ESG	250,000
Total Routes per ESG	250,000
Concurrent connections per ESG	1,000,000

The following table shows the limits for **Edge Services Gateway Quad-Large Maximums**:

Description	Limit
OSPF Routes per ESG	100,000
OSPF Adjacencies per ESG	40
BGP Peers per ESG	50
BGP Routes per ESG	250,000
Total Routes per ESG	250,000
Concurrent connections per ESG	1,000,000

The following table shows the limits for **Edge Services Gateway Overall Maximums**:

Description	Limit
Load Balancer VIPs	64
Load Balancer Pools	64
Load Balancer Servers per Pool	32
Firewall rules per ESG	2,000

The following table shows the limits for **DHCP: VPN Service Maximums**:

Description	Limit
DHCP Pools per Edge Service Gateway (all sizes)	20,000
Number of IPSEC tunnels per Edge gateway – Compact	512
Number of IPSEC tunnels per Edge gateway – Large	1,600
Number of IPSEC tunnels per Edge gateway – X-Large	4,096
Number of IPSEC tunnels per Edge gateway – Quad-Large	6,000
SSL VPN number of Concurrent connections (compact/large/x-large/quad-large)	50/100/100/1000

The following table shows the limits for **Multi-vCenter NSX Supported Features**:

Description	Limit
Logical Switch	Yes
L2 Bridges	No
Logical Distributed Router	Yes
Distributed Firewall	Yes
Edge Services	No
IP Security Groups	Yes

Summary

We started this chapter with an introduction to Network Virtualization and software-defined networking. We discussed the concepts of Network virtualization and introduced VMware's NSX Network virtualization platform. Then we discussed different NSX features and services, including logical switching, logical routing, edge gateway services, extensibility, service composer, and data security. Also, we briefly discussed the multi vCenter NSX feature. We ended the chapter with configuration maximums for NSX.

In the next chapter, we will discuss the core components that make up NSX. We will learn more about VXLAN architecture, Transport Zones and NSX Edge Gateways.

VTEP - VXLAN Tunnel Endpoint.

2
NSX Core Components

This chapter begins with a brief introduction of the NSX core components followed by a detailed discussion of these core components. We will go over three different control planes and see how each of the NSX core components fit in this architecture. Next, we will cover the VXLAN architecture and the transport zones that allow us to create and extend overlay networks across multiple clusters. We will also look at NSX Edge and the distributed firewall in greater detail and take a look at the newest NSX feature of multi-vCenter or cross-vCenter NSX deployment. By the end of this chapter, you will have a thorough understanding of the NSX core components and also their functional inter-dependencies.

In this chapter, we will cover the following topics:

- An introduction to the NSX core components
- NSX Manager
- NSX Controller clusters
- VXLAN architecture overview
- Transport zones
- NSX Edge
- Distributed firewall
- Cross-vCenter NSX

An introduction to the NSX core components

The foundational core components of NSX are divided across three different planes. The core components of a NSX deployment consist of an NSX Manager, Controller clusters, and **hypervisor kernel modules**. Each of these are crucial for your NSX deployment; however, they are decoupled to a certain extent to allow resiliency during the failure of multiple components. For example if your controller clusters fail, your virtual machines will still be able to communicate with each other without any network disruption.

 You have to ensure that the NSX components are always deployed in a clustered environment so that they are protected by vSphere HA.

The high-level architecture of NSX primarily describes three different planes wherein each of the core components fit in. They are the **Management plane**, the **Control plane,** and the **Data plane**. The following figure represents how the three planes are interlinked with each other. The management plane is how an end user interacts with NSX as a centralized access point, while the data plane consists of north-south or east-west traffic.

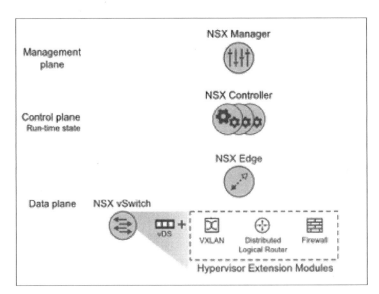

Let's look at some of the important components in the preceding figure:

- **Management plane**: The management plane primarily consists of NSX Manager. NSX Manager is a centralized network management component and primarily allows a single management point. It also provides the REST API that a user can use to perform all the NSX functions and actions. During the deployment phase, the management plane is established when the NSX appliance is deployed and configured. This management plane directly interacts with the control plane and also with the data plane. The NSX Manager is then managed via the vSphere web client and CLI. The NSX Manager is configured to interact with vSphere and ESXi, and once it's configured, all of the NSX components are then configured and managed via the vSphere web GUI.

- **Control plane**: The control plane consists of the NSX Controller that manages the state of virtual networks. NSX Controllers also enable overlay networks (VXLAN) that are multicast-free and make it easier to create new VXLAN networks without having to enable multicast functionality on physical switches. The controllers also keep track of all the information about the virtual machines, hosts, and VXLAN networks and can perform **Address Resolution Protocol (ARP)** suppression as well. No data passes through the control plane, and a loss of controllers does not affect network functionality between virtual machines.

 Overlay networks and VXLANs can be used interchangeably. They both represent L2 over L3 virtual networks.

- **Data plane**: The NSX data plane primarily consists of NSX **logical switch**. The NSX logical switch is a part of the vSphere distributed switch and is created when a VXLAN network is created. The logical switch and other NSX services such as logical routing and logical firewall are enabled at the hypervisor kernel level after the installation of hypervisor kernel modules (VIBs). This logical switch is the key to enabling **overlay networks** that are able to **encapsulate** and send traffic over existing physical networks. It also allows gateway devices that allow L2 bridging between virtual and physical workloads.

  The data plane receives its updates from the control plane as hypervisors maintain local virtual machines and **VXLAN** (Logical switch) mapping tables as well. A loss of data plane will cause a loss of the overlay (VXLAN) network, as virtual machines that are part of a NSX logical switch will not be able to send and receive data.

[VXLAN is discussed in greater detail ahead in this chapter.]

NSX Manager

NSX Manager, once deployed and configured, can deploy Controller cluster appliances and prepare the ESXi host that involves installing various **vSphere installation bundles (VIB)** that allow network virtualization features such as VXLAN, logical switching, logical firewall, and logical routing. NSX Manager can also deploy and configure Edge gateway appliances and its services.

[The NSX version as of this writing is 6.2 that only supports 1:1 vCenter connectivity.]

NSX Manager is deployed as a single virtual machine and relies on VMware's HA functionality to ensure its availability. There is no NSX Manager clustering available as of this writing. It is important to note that a loss of NSX Manager will lead to a loss of management and API access, but does not disrupt virtual machine connectivity.

Finally, the NSX Manager's configuration UI allows an administrator to collect log bundles and also to back up the NSX configuration.

NSX Controller clusters

NSX Controller provides a control plane functionality to distribute Logical Routing, VXLAN network information to the underlying hypervisor. Controllers are deployed as Virtual Appliances, and they should be deployed in the same vCenter to which NSX Manager is connected. In a production environment, it is recommended to deploy a minimum of three controllers. For better availability and scalability, we need to ensure that DRS anti-affinity rules are configured to deploy Controllers on a separate ESXI host. The control plane to management and data plane traffic is secured by a certificate-based authentication.

It is important to note that controller nodes employ a **scale-out mechanism**, where each controller node uses a **slicing** mechanism that divides the workload equally across all the nodes. This renders all the controller nodes as Active at all times. If one controller node fails, then the other nodes are reassigned the tasks that were owned by the failed node to ensure operational status. The VMware NSX Controller uses a **Paxos-based algorithm** within the NSX Controller cluster. The Controller removes dependency on multicast routing/PIM in the physical network. It also suppresses broadcast traffic in VXLAN networks.

The NSX version 6.2 only supports three controller nodes.

VXLAN architecture overview

One of the most important functions of NSX is enabling virtual networks. These virtual networks or overlay networks have become very popular due to the fact that they can leverage existing network infrastructure without the need to modify it in any way. The decoupling of logical networks from the physical infrastructure allows users to scale rapidly. Overlay networks or **Virtual Extensible Local Area Network (VXLAN)** was developed by a host of vendors that include Arista, Cisco, Citrix, Red Hat, and Broadcom. Due to this joint effort in developing its architecture, it allows the VXLAN standard to be implemented by multiple vendors.

VXLAN is a **layer 2 over layer 3 tunneling** protocol that allows logical network segments to extend on routable networks. This is achieved by encapsulating the **Ethernet frame** with additional **UPD, IP**, and **VXLAN headers**. Consequently, this increases the size of the packet by 50 bytes. Hence, VMware recommends increasing the MTU size to a minimum of 1600 bytes for all the interfaces in the physical infrastructure and any associated vSwitches.

When a virtual machine generates traffic meant for another virtual machine on the same virtual network, the hosts on which these source and destination virtual machines run are called **VXLAN Tunnel End Point (VTEP)**. VTEPs are configured as separate VM Kernel interfaces on the hosts. The outer IP header block in the VXLAN frame contains the source and the destination IP addresses that contain the source hypervisor and the destination hypervisor. When a packet leaves the source virtual machine, it is encapsulated at the source hypervisor and sent to the target hypervisor. The target hypervisor, upon receiving this packet, **decapsulates** the Ethernet frame and forwards the packet to the destination virtual machine.

Once the ESXI host is prepared from NSX Manager, we need to configure VTEP. NSX supports multiple VXLAN vmknics per host for uplink load balancing features. In addition to this, **Guest VLAN tagging** is also supported.

RFC

A sample packet flow

We face a challenging situation when a virtual machine generates traffic—**Broadcast, Unknown Unicast, or Multicast (BUM)**—meant for another virtual machine on the same **Virtual Network Identifier (VNI)** on a different host. Control plane modes play a crucial factor in optimizing the VXLAN traffic depending on the modes selected for the Logical Switch/Transport Scope:

- Unicast
- Hybrid
- Multicast

By default, a Logical Switch inherits its **replication mode** from the transport zone. However, we can set this on a per-Logical-Switch basis. Segment ID is needed for Multicast and Hybrid Modes.

 We will look at setting this replication mode when we configure the transport zones.

The following is a representation of the VXLAN-encapsulated packet showing the VXLAN headers:

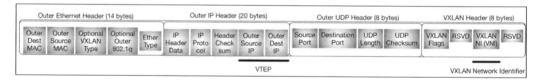

As indicated in the preceding figure, the outer IP header identifies the source and the destination VTEPs. The VXLAN header also has the **Virtual Network Identifier (VNI)** that is a 24-bit unique network identifier. This allows the scaling of virtual networks beyond the 4094 VLAN limitation placed by the physical switches. Two virtual machines that are a part of the same virtual network will have the same virtual network identifier, similar to how two machines on the same VLAN share the same VLAN ID.

 You can create up to 16777215 VXLAN segments in NSX.

Transport zones

A group of ESXi hosts that are able to communicate with one another over the physical network by means of VTEPs are said to be in the same transport zone. A transport zone defines the extension of a logical switch across multiple ESXi clusters that span across multiple virtual distributed switches.

A typical environment has more than one virtual distributed switch that spans across multiple hosts. A transport zone enables a logical switch to extend across multiple virtual distributed switches, and any ESXi host that is a part of this transport zone can have virtual machines as a part of that logical network. A logical switch is always created as part of a transport zone and ESXi hosts can participate in them.

The following is a figure that shows a transport zone that defines the extension of a logical switch across multiple virtual distributed switches:

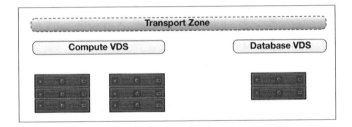

NSX Edge Services Gateway

The NSX **Edge Services Gateway (ESG)** offers a feature rich set of services that include NAT, routing, firewall, load balancing, L2/L3 VPN, and DHCP/DNS relay. NSX API allows each of these services to be deployed, configured, and consumed on-demand.

The ESG is deployed as a virtual machine from NSX Manager that is accessed using the vSphere web client. Four different form factors are offered for differently-sized environments. It is important that you factor in enough resources for the appropriate ESG when building your environment.

The ESG can be deployed in different sizes. The following are the available size options for an ESG appliance:

- **X-Large**: The X-large form factor is suitable for high performance firewall, load balancer, and routing or a combination of multiple services. When an X-large form factor is selected, the ESG will be deployed with six vCPUs and 8GB of RAM.

- **Quad-Large**: The Quad-large form factor is ideal for a high performance firewall. It will be deployed with four vCPUs and 1GB of RAM.

- **Large**: The large form factor is suitable for medium performance routing and firewall. It is recommended that, in production, you start with the large form factor. The large ESG is deployed with two vCPUs and 1GB of RAM.

- **Compact**: The compact form factor is suitable for DHCP and DNS replay functions. It is deployed with one vCPU and 512MB of RAM.

Once deployed, a form factor can be upgraded by using the API or the UI. The upgrade action will incur an outage. We will look at upgrading the form factor in more detail in the following chapters. Edge gateway services can also be deployed in an Active/Standby mode to ensure high availability and resiliency. A **heartbeat network** between the Edge appliances ensures state replication and uptime. If the active gateway goes down and the "declared dead time" passes, the standby Edge appliance takes over.

 The default declared dead time is 15 seconds and can be reduced to 6 seconds.

Let's look at some of the Edge services as follows:

- **Network Address Translation**: The NSX Edge supports both source and destination NAT and NAT is allowed for all traffic flowing through the Edge appliance. If the Edge appliance supports more than 100 virtual machines, it is recommended that a Quad instance be deployed to allow high performance translation.

- **Routing**: The NSX Edge allows centralized routing that allows the logical networks deployed in the NSX domain to be routed to the external physical network. The Edge supports multiple routing protocols including **OSPF**, **iBGP**, and **eBGP**. The Edge also supports static routing.

- **Load balancing**: The NSX Edge also offers a load balancing functionality that allows the load balancing of traffic between the virtual machines. The load balancer supports different balancing mechanisms including IP Hash, least connections, URI-based, and round robin.

- **Firewall**: NSX Edge provides a stateful firewall functionality that is ideal for north-south traffic flowing between the physical and the virtual workloads behind the Edge gateway. The Edge firewall can be deployed alongside the hypervisor kernel-based distributed firewall that is primarily used to enforce security policies between workloads in the same logical network.

- **L2/L3VPN**: The Edge also provides L2 and L3 VPNs that makes it possible to extend L2 domains between two sites. An IPSEC site-to-site connectivity between two NSX Edges or other VPN termination devices can also be set up.

- **DHCP/DNS relay**: NSX Edge also offers DHCP and DNS relay functions that allows you to offload these services to the Edge gateway. Edge only supports DNS relay functionality and can forward any DNS requests to the DNS server. The Edge gateway can be configured as a DHCP server to provide and manage IP addresses, default gateway, DNS servers and, search domain information for workloads connected to the logical networks.

Distributed firewall

NSX provides **L2-L4stateful firewall** services by means of a distributed firewall that runs in the ESXi hypervisor kernel. Because the firewall is a function of the ESXi kernel, it provides massive throughput and performs at a near line rate. When the ESXi host is initially prepared by NSX, the distributed firewall service is installed in the kernel by deploying the kernel **VIB – VMware Internetworking Service** insertion platform or VSIP. VSIP is responsible for monitoring and enforcing security policies on all the traffic flowing through the data plane. The **distributed firewall (DFW)** throughput and performance scales horizontally as more ESXi hosts are added.

DFW instances are associated to each vNIC, and every vNIC requires one DFW instance. A virtual machine with two vNICs has two DFW instances associated with it, each monitoring its own vNIC and applying security policies to it. DFW is ideally deployed to protect virtual-to-virtual or virtual-to-physical traffic. This makes DFW very effective in protecting east-west traffic between workloads that are a part of the same logical network. DFW policies can also be used to restrict traffic between virtual machines and external networks because it is applied at the vNIC of the virtual machine. Any virtual machine that does not require firewall protection can be added to the exclusion list.

A diagrammatic representation is shown as follows:

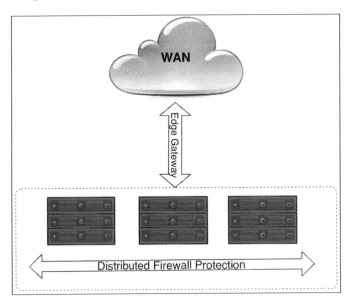

DFW fully supports **vMotion** and the rules applied to a virtual machine always follow the virtual machine. This means any manual or automated vMotion triggered by DRS does not cause any disruption in its protection status.

The **VSIP kernel module** also adds **spoofguard** and traffic redirection functionalities as well. The spoofguard function maintains a VM name and IP address-mapping table and prevents against IP spoofing. Spoofguard is disabled by default and needs to be manually enabled per logical switch or virtual distributed switch port group. Traffic redirection allows traffic to be redirected to a third-party appliance that can do enhanced monitoring, if needed. This allows third-party vendors to be interfaced with DFW directly and offer custom services as needed. We will discuss this further in the following chapters.

Cross-vCenter NSX

With NSX 6.2, VMware introduced an interesting feature that allows you to manage multiple vCenter NSX environments using a primary NSX Manager. This allows for easy management and also enables lots of new functionalities including extending networks and other features such as distributed logical routing. Cross-vCenter NSX deployment also allows centralized management and eases disaster recovery architectures.

In a cross-vCenter deployment, multiple vCenters are all paired with their own NSX Manager per vCenter. One NSX Manager is assigned as the primary while other NSX Managers become secondary. This primary NSX Manager can now deploy a universal controller cluster that provides the control plane. Unlike a standalone vCenter-NSX deployment, secondary NSX Managers do not deploy their own controller clusters.

The primary NSX Manager also creates objects whose scope is universal. This means that these objects extend to all the secondary NSX Managers. These universal objects are synchronized across all the secondary NSX Managers and can be edited and changed by the primary NSX Manager only. This does not prevent you from creating local objects on each of the NSX Managers.

Similar to local NSX objects, a primary NSX Manager can create global objects such as **universal transport zones**, **universal logical switches**, **universal distributed routers**, **universal firewall rules**, and **universal security objects**. There can be only one universal transport zone in a cross-vCenter NSX environment. After it is created, it is synchronized across all the secondary NSX Managers. When a logical switch is created inside a universal transport zone, it becomes a universal logical switch that spans layer 2 network across all the vCenters. All traffic is routed using the universal logical router, and any traffic that needs to be routed between a universal logical switch and a logical switch (local scope) requires an ESG. We will discuss the features of this in the upcoming chapters.

Summary

We began the chapter with a brief introduction of the NSX core components and looked at the management, control, and the data plane. We then discussed NSX Manager and the NSX Controller clusters. This was followed by a VXLAN architecture overview discussion, where we looked at the VXLAN packet. We then discussed transport zones and NSX Edge gateway services. We ended the chapter with NSX Distributed firewall services and also an overview of Cross-vCenter NSX deployment.

In the next chapter, we will start deploying our NSX environment and deploy all of its components starting with NSX Manager. We will configure NSX Manager using its user interface and build our control plane by deploying controller clusters.

3
NSX Installation and Configuration

This chapter describes the step-by-step installation of NSX and its configuration. We will begin by getting our environment ready for NSX and then go over downloading and deploying NSX. We will then cover the NSX Manager management interface and configure it with our vCenter and license it. We will spend time getting to know the NSX user interface in the vSphere web client and build a control plane by deploying controller clusters. This will be followed by our data plane preparation, which involves preparing the ESXi clusters for network virtualization.

In this chapter, we will cover the following topics:

- Preparing your environment
- Downloading and deploying NSX Manager
- An overview of the NSX Manager interface
- Configuring NSX Manager
- Managing NSX using the vSphere web client
- Deploying the control plane (Controller Virtual Machines)
- Deploying the data plane
- Licensing

Preparing your environment

Before installing NSX, it is important to understand its requirements. NSX Manager and its related components require a considerable amount of resources, and planning ahead is very important. The following is a table that lists the minimum resource requirements for NSX Manager and its related components.

Component	CPU	Memory	Disk Space
NSX Manager	4vCPU	16GB	60GB
NSX Controller	4vCPU	4GB	20GB
NSX Edge	1 vCPU (Compact) 2 vCPU (Large) 4 vCPU (Quad Large) 6 vCPU (X-Large)	512MB (Compact) 1GB (Large/Quad Large) 8GB (X-Large)	512MB (Compact/Large/Quad-Large) 4.5 GB (X-Large)

You also need to have vCenter 5.5 or later installed in your environment with each server running ESXi version 5.5 or newer. Multi-vCenter deployment will require vCenter version 6.0. NSX also requires a range of ports to be allowed in your network. We will need TCP port 80 and 443 open for vSphere communication and the NSX REST API functionality. We also need TCP ports 1234, 5671, and 22 for host to controller cluster communication, the RabbitMQ message bus, and SSH console access, respectively. You will also need virtual distributed switches (version 5.5 and above) in your environment, which is the foundation for VXLAN logical segments.

> Remember **not to upgrade** the VMware tools on each NSX appliance as a specific functionality is tied to each version of these tools. Upgrading without official VMware guidance can potentially break your NSX deployment.

Downloading and deploying NSX Manager

NSX Manager is an appliance and can be downloaded online from VMware's website. The download is available in an OVA format that can be deployed in your environment. Before discussing the deployment of NSX, let's go over some of the deployment considerations for NSX.

VMware recommends that NSX Manager be deployed on a separate management cluster, which will be separate from the compute cluster where your software-defined networks will be deployed. This **decouples** the management plane from the compute plane, which is necessary, and allows you to have a higher availability of your management systems. The management cluster will also run the vCenter server, and NSX controllers are deployed in the compute cluster. The controller cluster virtual machines should be deployed in the management network and should be able to reach the vCenter server and hypervisors. It is also important to recall that vCenter and NSX have a 1:1 relationship, with one NSX Manager connected to only one vCenter.

 NSX Manager deploys controller instances on the clusters managed by the NSX-registered vCenter. You cannot deploy controller instances to a cluster that is not registered by NSX Manager.

It is also important to size the environment appropriately to allow easy resource additions, if needed. Also, NSX Manager does not have a built-in HA functionality and relies on ESXi's HA and DRS features to avoid downtime and resource contention. A minimum of three nodes is recommended for the management cluster to run NSX Manager. The management cluster should also be completely separate from any IP addressing space that is chosen to run compute production instances (instances such as your web, database, and application footprints), thereby keeping the management and compute planes isolated.

Once the NSX Manager OVA file is downloaded, we will proceed to import it to our vSphere cluster as shown here.

 Deployment can be done using the Windows-based vSphere client or vSphere web client. Because NSX can only be managed using the web client, we will deploy it using the web client, which is usually preferred.

1. Get to the OVF deployment screen by clicking on **Hypervisors and Clusters**. Expand vCenter, right-click on the hypervisor, and select **Deploy OVF Template...**:

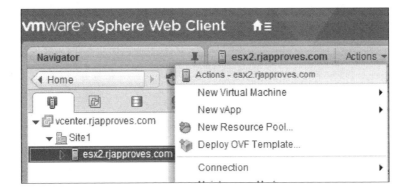

2. You will see the **Deploy OVF Template** screen:

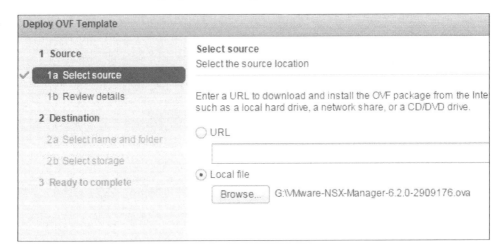

3. Select the OVF/OVA package that you have downloaded and click on **Next**. You will see the details of the NSX OVA next. Accept the extra configurations by clicking in the checkbox and then click on **Next**:

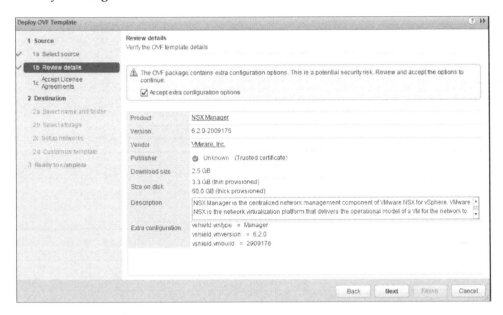

4. Accept the EULA by clicking on the **Accept** button and then click on **Next**:

5. Name your NSX Manager instance and select the datacenter or folder where you want it to be deployed. Click on **Next** to proceed to the next screen:

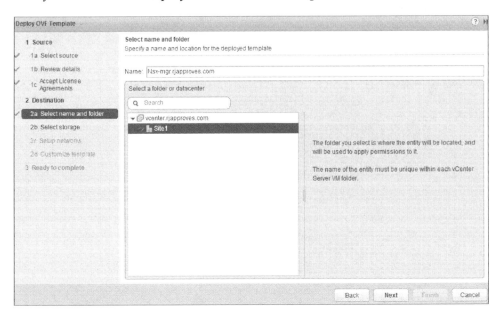

6. Next, select the storage location and the appropriate policy. The default disk format is **Thick Provision Lazy Zeroed** but I am going to deploy this appliance in a thin disk format to conserve space in my lab:

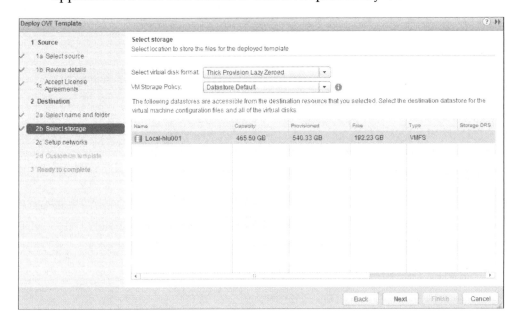

7. Select the network on which this NSX Manager will be deployed. Typically, this will be a management network where NSX Manager is able to connect and talk to vCenter. Click on **Next**:

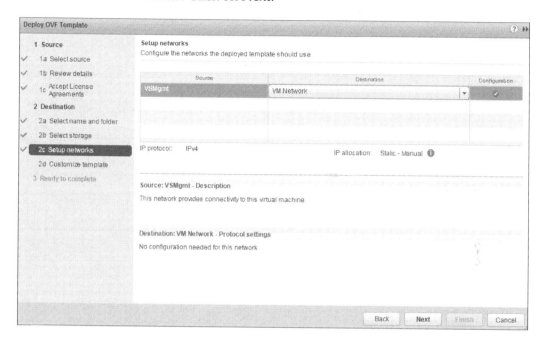

8. Now, you will have to input all the values with which to configure this appliance. This includes a CLI admin and privileged mode passwords, IP address assignments, DNS, and NTP settings as well. There is an option to enable SSH mode; however, in production environments, this is not the best practice unless you have taken appropriate measures to secure SSH access. Leaving the IP section blank will invoke a DHCP request to your DHCP server.

 Please Note: Ensure that forward and reverse DNS entries are in place in your DNS server.

9. As seen in the following screenshot, click on **Next** once you have filled all the values appropriately:

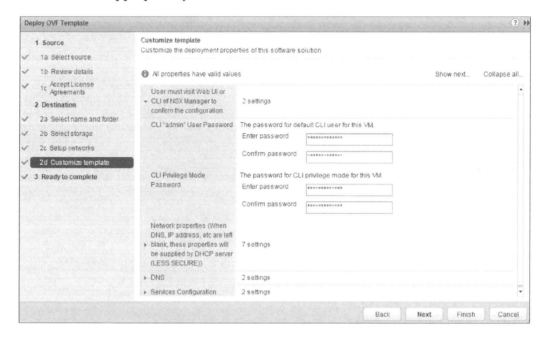

10. Review the summary page and click on **Finish:**

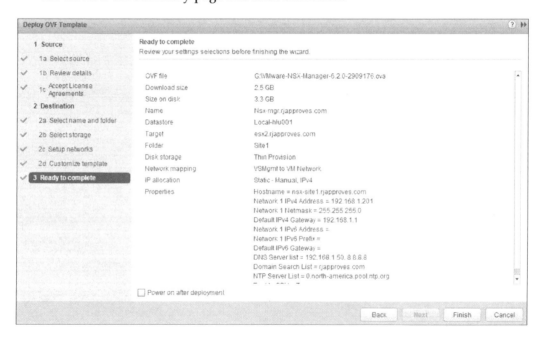

11. You will now see your NSX Manager being deployed in the tasks pane:

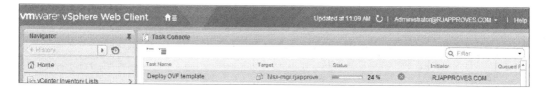

An overview of the NSX Manager interface

Once NSX Manager is successfully deployed, you should be able to see it in your inventory:

1. Click on the NSX Manager virtual machine and review the **Summary** tab:

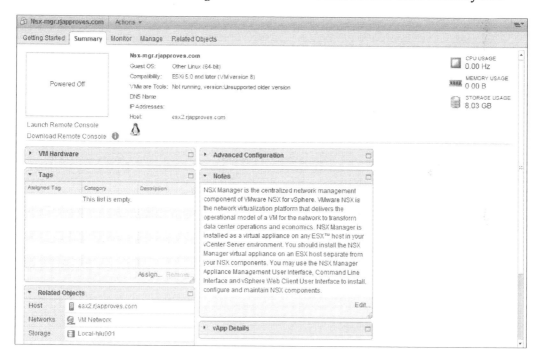

2. You should be able to see that the NSX virtual machine adds notes to the summary page. You will also see that this virtual machine took up about 8 GB of disk space initially because I opted to deploy it in thin disk mode.

3. Let's click on the **Manage** tab to review default hardware requirements:

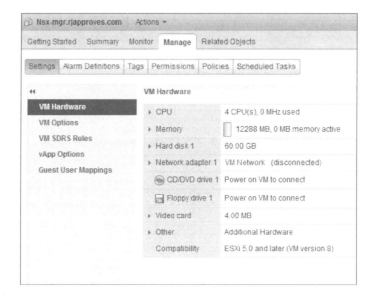

4. The NSX Manager virtual machine has been allocated four CPUs and about 16 GB of RAM. The hard disk is set to be 60 GB in size.

5. Let's proceed to power on this virtual machine. Right–click on the NSX Manager virtual machine by navigating to **Power** | **Power On**.

6. You will now see that NSX is powered on and the VMware guest tools have been started:

7. Let's access NSX Manager from the browser and review its interface and options. Open up a new browser or a new tab and enter the FQDN or the IP address of NSX Manager. The NSX Manager web interface is accessed over SSL:

8. Log in to NSX Manager with the admin username and the password that was set during deployment time. Once logged in, you will see the splash page that allows you to configure your appliance:

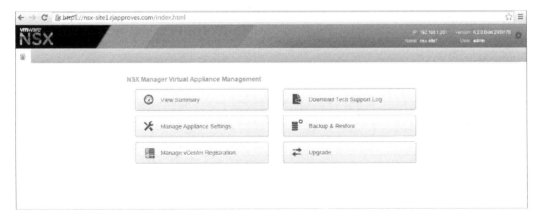

9. Clicking on the **View Summary** tab seen in the preceding screenshot gives you the summary of the current state of the NSX Manager appliance. This includes resource consumptions and a service status:

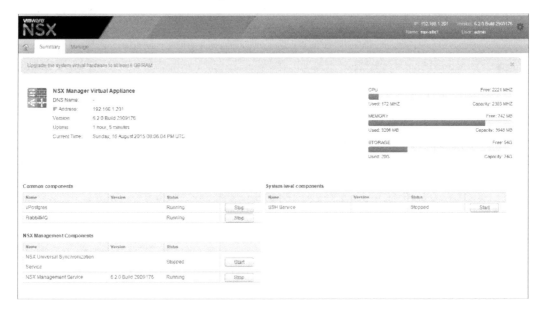

10. To enable SSH access to the manager, simply click on the **Start** button and the service will be started.

11. The **Manage** tab allows you to manage and configure NSX Manager:

12. Some of the things that you can configure include a syslog server, network, SSL certificates, and backup and restore; you can also upgrade the appliance. We will learn more about these in the upcoming chapters.

The NSX management service allows you to configure NSX Manager with a Virtual Center and a lookup service:

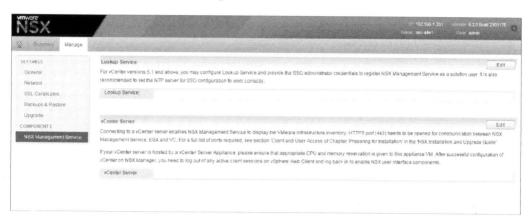

13. Lastly, to log out of your NSX Manager, click on the gear symbol in the upper-right corner and then click on the **Logout** option:

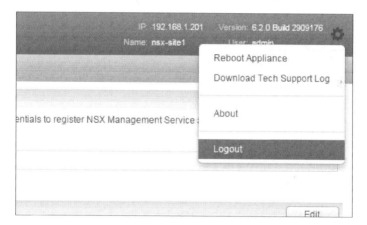

Configuring the NSX Manager

Now that we have deployed the NSX Manager and had a quick overview of it, let's go ahead and configure this manager with our vCenter server.

 The vCenter Server version in my environment is 6.0. The lookup service port in the 6.x vCenter version is 443.

1. Once you are logged into the NSX Manager, click on **Manage.** Under the **Components** section, click on **NSX Management Service:**

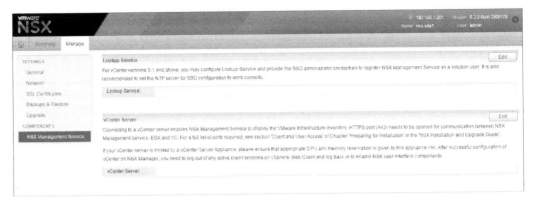

2. Under the **vCenter Server** section, click on **Edit**. You will see the following screen:

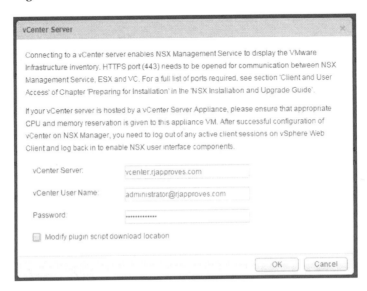

3. Enter your **vCenter Server** FQDN and a username and password. Click on **OK** when done.

 It is best practice to create a custom user for NSX Manager. You have built-in roles such as Enterprise administrator, NSX administrator, and Security administrator. We will explore this further in the users and roles chapter.

4. Accept the SSL certificate by clicking on **Yes**:

5. Once connected, you will see a connected status:

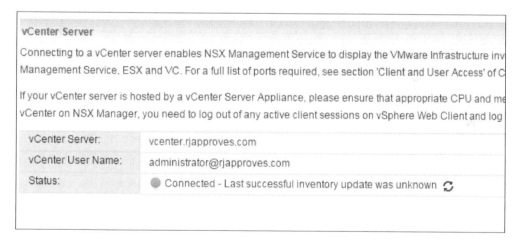

6. To use SSO on NSX Manager, you should have the SSO service installed on vCenter. Click on **Edit** in the lookup service section and fill out your SSO service credentials. Accept the SSL certificate prompts:

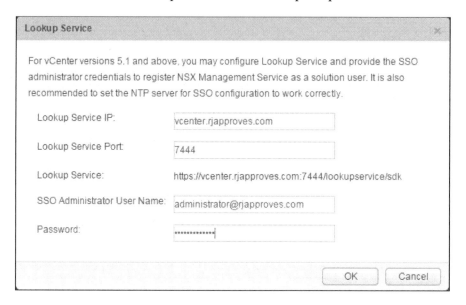

7. Once connected, you will see a status update as shown in the following screenshot:

8. We have now configured our NSX Manager with a vCenter server.

Managing NSX using the vSphere web client

NSX can only be managed using the vSphere web client. When NSX is configured with vCenter, it installs a plugin for the web client. There is no management functionality available in the classic Windows client.

 If you are already logged in, you will need to log out and log back in to the vSphere web client after about 5 minutes for the plugin to show up.

Once logged in to your vSphere web client, you will see a new icon called **Networking & Security**. You will see this on the left-hand side navigation pane as well:

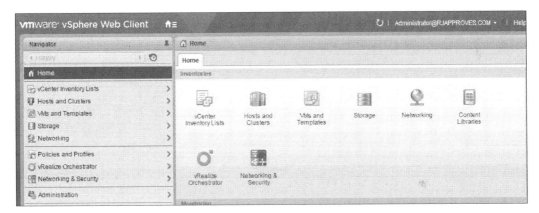

Now, perform the following steps to generate a license:

1. Click on the icon or the option and you should see the following screen:

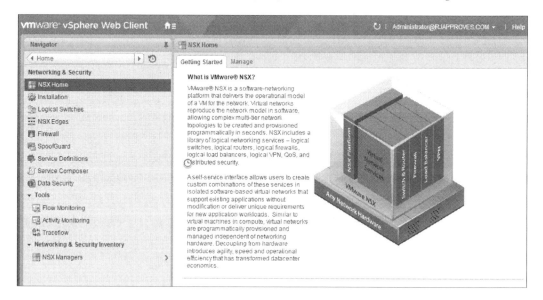

2. There are many menu items but let's click on **NSX Managers** under **Networking & Security Inventory**. This shows us the NSX Manager that is registered:

3. Clicking on the NSX Manager allows you to view the **current licensing status** and to manage and monitor the NSX Manager:

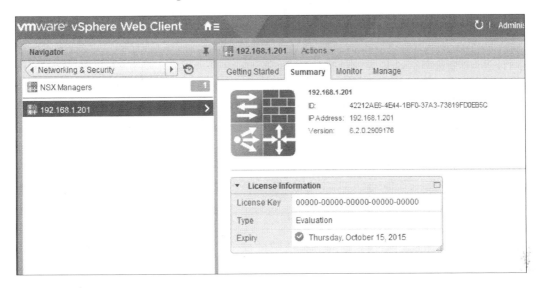

4. Before we begin to set up the control plane and prepare our clusters for Network virtualization, let's add the appropriate **licensing** for NSX. NSX, by default, allows you to have up to **60 days of license-free usage**.

5. Log in to the web client and navigate to **Administration | Licenses | Assets | Solutions**:

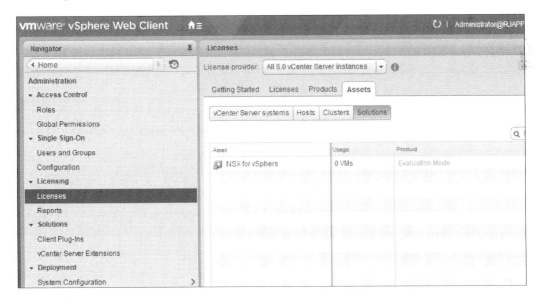

6. Click on **NSX for vSphere** and click on the **Assign License...** button:

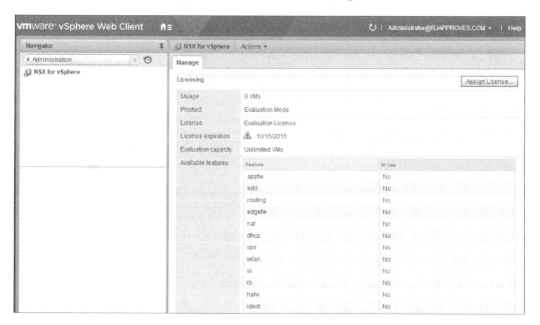

7. In the **License** view, click on the + symbol to open up the licensing window:

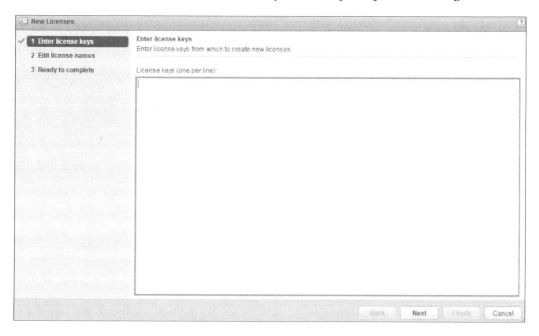

8. Copy and paste or type in your license key and click on **Next**:

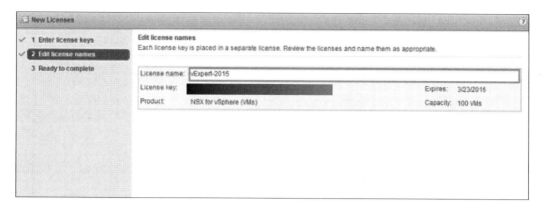

9. Click on **Finish** when you are ready. Make sure you select the NSX license from the licensing options:

Deploying the control plane

The control plane consists of the **controller nodes** that eliminate the need for multicast support from the physical network infrastructure to manage VXLAN-based logical switches. A minimum of **three controller virtual machines** are required for high availability.

To deploy controller nodes, go to **Networking & Security | Installation**, and under the **Management** tab, click on the + symbol in the NSX Controller nodes section.

In this lab environment, we will be only deploying one controller node. VMware recommends that you add three controllers for scale and redundancy. Controller cluster virtual machines employ a **slicing mechanism**, meaning all of them are active at any given time. If a controller virtual machine fails, the tasks failover to the other active peers. This is done by means of a master controller that is elected by means of a majority vote. To maintain this majority, it is always recommended to deploy controller cluster virtual machines in odd numbers.

Ensure ample resources in the cluster while deploying the controller nodes. You cannot modify resources for the controller nodes.

Perform the following steps to add a controller:

1. Select the appropriate options for **NSX Manager, Datacenter, Cluster/ Resource Pool, Datastore**, desired **Host** if any, **Folder** if any, and the network port group as well. The network port group can be a logical switch, port group, or distributed port group. The controller node must be reachable by the NSX Manager and the vSphere hosts with which it has to communicate. Usually, controller nodes are part of the management network.

2. Click on **Select** to define the IP pool that is a range of predetermined IP addresses. These IPs should be able to reach vCenter and the management network including the compute hypervisors. The controller node, when deployed, gets an IP allocated from this pool of IPs. The following screenshot shows the **Select IP Pool** window:

3. Click on **New IP Pool...** and fill in the values appropriately. The IP range needs to be added and sized appropriately to accommodate the number of controller nodes you plan to deploy:

4. Click on **OK** when done, and you will see the pool in the list of available pools.

5. Click it to select the pool and press **OK**:

6. Next, enter the password and click on **OK**.

   The password must contain eight characters and must follow three of the following four rules:

   ° At least one uppercase letter

   ° At least one lowercase letter

   ° At last one number

   ° At least one special character

7. When done, you will now see that the controller node is being deployed with the **Deploying** status shown:

8. You can also monitor the controller node progress in the **Recent Tasks** pane:

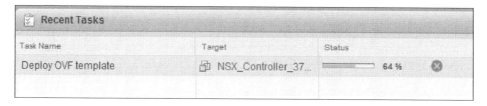

9. Once deployed, you will see the NSX Controller in the host as shown in the following screenshot. The NSX Manager will continue to power on the controller node once the deployment is complete:

10. The controller status in the NSX Manager gets updated once the controller node is powered on and ready to be used:

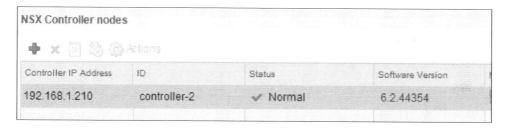

Deploying the data plane

Deploying the data plane involves **preparing** the ESXi hosts that enable them to participate in network virtualization. To prepare your environment for network virtualization, network components must be installed on a per-cluster basis. Any new hypervisors added to this cluster will automatically be prepared for network virtualization. After the network virtualization software (installed as a VIB) is installed, a logical firewall is enabled on that cluster. One important prerequisite is to ensure that all hosts in the cluster are part of the distributed virtual switch.

> **Please note**: You must ensure that all hosts in the cluster are part of the distributed virtual switch.

1. To prepare a cluster, navigate to **Networking & Security | Installation |** and then go to the **Host Preparation** tab:

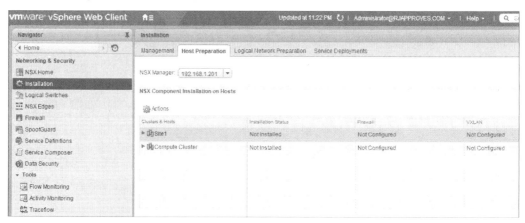

2. I will be preparing the **Compute Cluster** that consists of only one host. Hover on the installation status column and you will find the **Install** option:

3. Click on **Install**. Click on **Yes** in the prompt to proceed. You will now see the **Installing** status:

 Although not necessary, in rare instances a reinstall would require the ESXi host to reboot.

4. Once the installation is complete, you will see the status updated and the distributed firewall enabled:

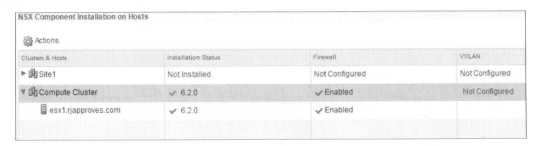

5. All hosts in the Compute cluster will have three VIBs installed. The installed VIBs prepare the hosts in the cluster for logical routing, VXLAN, and distributed firewall. You can log in to a host and run the following command to find the installed VIBs:

```
[root@host:~] esxcli software vib list | grepesx
esx-vsip6.0.0-0.0.2732470     VMware  VMwareCertified  2015-05-29
esx-vxlan6.0.0-0.0.2732470    VMware  VMwareCertified  2015-05-29
```

Summary

We began this chapter by preparing our environment and understanding the different limitations of NSX in order to begin its deployment. We then went ahead and deployed the NSX Manager using the vSphere web client. Remember that NSX cannot be managed by the traditional Windows client and can only be managed by the vSphere web client. We then had a quick overview of the NSX Manager to familiarize ourselves with the management interface functionality. Next, we went ahead and configured our NSX Manager with our vCenter server. This allowed us to start the configuration of the NSX services for our vCenter. We managed our NSX Manager using the vSphere web client and continued to deploy our control plane. Lastly, we prepared our hosts for network virtualization by deploying the data plane that, by default, enables the distributed firewall service on all ESXi hosts in a cluster.

In the next chapter, we will go over the step-by-step deployment and configuration of multiple NSX features and services and configure logical switches, transport zones, and other NSX functions.

4
NSX Functional Services

In this chapter, we will go over the step-by-step deployment and configuration of multiple NSX features and services. In the previous chapter, we got our environment ready by downloading and deploying NSX. We also configured the NSX Manager, built our control plane, and deployed the controller clusters that were followed by preparing our hosts for network virtualization. This now leaves us with an environment in which we can go ahead and configure primary and secondary NSX Managers, Transport Zones, logical switching, L2 bridges, logical routers, and firewall, and we can take a look at the Edge services gateway as well.

In this chapter, we will cover the following topics:

- Primary and secondary NSX Managers
- Transport Zones
- Logical switching
- L2 bridges
- Deploying a NSX Edge logical router
- The Edge services gateway
- The logical firewall

Primary and secondary NSX Managers

In the earlier chapters, we discussed cross-vCenter NSX deployment. We will now look at the configuration of primary and secondary NSX Managers in a multi-vCenter NSX deployment.

As of NSX 6.2, there can be one primary NSX Manager and up to seven secondary NSX Managers. You can select one primary NSX Manager, following which you can start creating universal objects and can deploy universal controller clusters as well. The **universal controller cluster** will provide the control plane for the cross-vCenter NSX environment. Remember that in a cross-vCenter environment, the secondary NSX Managers do not have their own controller clusters.

> **Please note**: As of NSX 6.2, there can be one primary NSX Manager and up to seven secondary NSX Managers.

Before assigning a primary role to an NSX Manager, ensure that it has the controller clusters deployed, prepared, and configured.

1. Log in to the vCenter web portal and go to **Home | Networking & Security | Installation** and select the **Management** tab.

2. Select the NSX Manager to which you want to assign a primary role and click on **Actions | Assign Primary Role**:

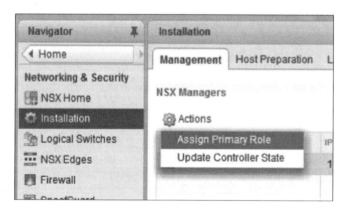

This assigns the primary role to the NSX Manager.

Once you have an NSX Manager as a primary, you can now log in to a secondary NSX Manager. Ensure that no controller cluster is deployed at the NSX Manager that is going to be assigned a secondary role.

1. Log in to vCenter that is linked to the primary NSX Manager.

2. Go to **Home | Networking & Security | Installation** and select the **Management** tab.

3. Click on the primary NSX Manager and then go to **Actions | Add Secondary NSX Manager**:

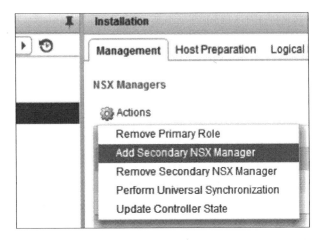

4. Enter the IP address, user name, and password of the secondary NSX Manager and click on **OK**:

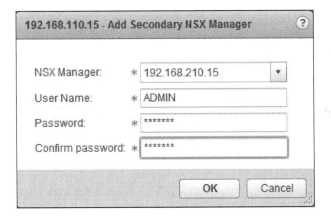

5. Check the certificate and upon registration, you will now have a secondary NSX Manager configured.

Now that we have the primary and secondary managers configured, we can proceed to creating universal objects in the primary NSX Manager that spans the multisite cross-vCenter environment.

Transport Zones

We have briefly looked at what Transport Zones are in the previous chapters. A Transport Zone controls the domain of a logical switch among hosts. In other words, a Transport Zone controls which clusters (hosts) can be part of a logical switch. A Transport Zone is configured on a cluster by cluster basis and can span multiple clusters in vCenter. A **Universal Transport Zone** can span multiple clusters over multiple vCenters. A Transport Zone dictates which host and by extension which virtual machines are allowed to participate in a particular network. In a typical environment, there can be more than one Transport Zone that is mapped to a host or to a cluster. However, a logical switch can belong to only one Transport Zone.

[

Please note: A logical switch can belong to only one Transport Zone.
]

If a virtual machine belongs to a different Transport Zone, you will not be able to directly communicate with that virtual machine. This means that **virtualized Network Interface Card (vNIC)** is limited the bounds of a Transport Zone. A virtual machine, however, can have multiple vNICs, each belonging to a different Transport Zone.

In a cross-vCenter NSX environment, you create a Universal Transport Zone that includes clusters from any vCenter in the entire environment, thereby extending your logical network. However, you can create only one Universal Transport Zone.

A Universal Transport Zone is created by the primary NSX Manager and is replicated to all the secondary NSX Managers. A universal logical switch associated with a Universal Transport Zone can extend to one or more vSphere clusters across multiple vCenters. There can be only one Universal Transport Zone.

[

Please note: As of NSX 6.2, you can create only one Universal Transport Zone.
]

To add a Transport Zone, do the following:

1. Go to **Home | Networking & Security | Installation | Logical Network Preparation | Transport Zones**.

2. Click on the + icon to add a new Transport Zone. To add a Universal Transport Zone in a cross-vCenter NSX environment, you have to select the primary NSX Manager, as shown in the following screenshot:

3. Enabling **Mark this object for Universal Synchronization** allows this to be a Universal Transport Zone.

4. Name the Transport Zone appropriately.

5. Select a replication mode.

    ° **Multicast**: Instead of deploying controller clusters, you can use multicast IP addresses in the physical network for your control plane in this mode. This mode requires **Protocol Independent Multicast (PIM)/Internet Group Management Protocol (IGMP)** to be configured in your physical network.

    ° **Unicast**: The control plane is managed by NSX by means of controller clusters. No changes are needed in the physical network.

    ° **Hybrid**: The hybrid mode offloads any local traffic replication to the physical network by means of multicast. This requires IGMP snooping to be configured in your physical network.

Remember to watch out for **overlapping multicast addresses** in a cross-vCenter NSX environment. The recommended multicast address range starts at 239.0.1.0/24 and excludes 239.128.0.0/24. The range 239.128.0.0/24 should not be used, as this range is used for local subnet control that can cause the physical switch to flood all the traffic that uses this address range.

1. Select the clusters across which you want this Transport Zone to span. A Transport Zone will remain local to the NSX Manager in which it was created. A Universal Transport Zone will span all the NSX environments in a cross-vCenter NSX deployment. Click on **OK** when done. The following screenshot shows some of the Transport Zones:

2. The Transport Zone is now created. Notice the scope and icon differences between a global and a Universal Transport Zone.

You can double-click on the Transport Zone to manage its settings. Alternatively, you can choose the **Actions** dropdown to change its settings. You can also add or remove any clusters from the Transport Zone membership as required.

Logical switching

Logical switches have similar functionality to that of a physical switch—they allow the isolation of your applications and tenants for security and other purposes. A logical switch creates a **broadcast domain** to allow such an isolation of virtual machines. Using logical switches, you can now not only create VLANs that are similar to a physical switch, but also make them span across large compute clusters. This now allows you to migrate your virtual machines using vMotion without range limitations of the physical network. The logical switch is mapped to a VXLAN that encapsulates the traffic over the physical network. We discussed VXLAN and its packet architecture in *Chapter 2, NSX Core Components*.

Logical switches are local to a virtual center NSX deployment; however, you can create a universal logical switch that can span across vCenters, which can effectively extend your VXLAN across two different sites.

The NSX controller maintains information about all virtual machines, hosts, logical switches, and its VXLANs.

The following are the prerequisites for creating a logical switch:

- vSphere distributed switches must be configured. You cannot deploy logical switches on standard switches.
- NSX controllers must be deployed.
- Your compute host clusters must be prepared and ready to go.
- VXLAN must be configured.
- A Transport Zone and a segment ID pool must be configured.

Let's also look at some prerequisites for creating a universal logical switch for a multi-vCenter NSX environment:

- vSphere distributed switches must be configured on both sides
- The NSX Manager and NSX controllers must be deployed on both vCenters.
- On both sites, hosts must be prepared and VXLAN must be configured.
- A primary NSX Manager must be assigned
- A universal segment ID pool and a Universal Transport Zone must be configured

To configure a logical switch, perform the following set of steps:

1. Open up your vSphere web client and navigate to **Home | Networking & Security | Logical Switches**.
2. From the **NSX Manager** drop-down menu, select the NSX Manager where you want to set up your logical switch.

3. To create a universal logical switch, you must select the primary NSX Manager. If the enhanced vCenter linked mode is configured, you will be able to select and manage multiple NSX Managers from any vCenter; however, one NSX Manager can only be associated with one vCenter:

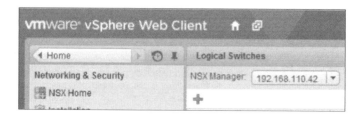

4. Click on the **+** sign to add a new logical switch:

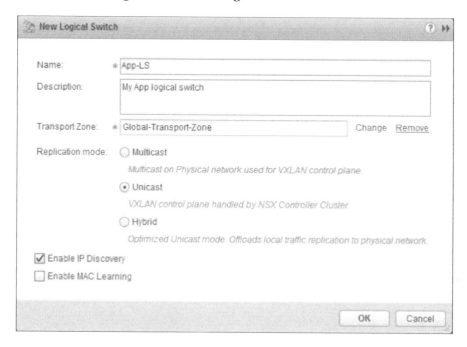

5. Enter **Name** of your logical switch.

6. Enter **Description** (optional).

7. Select **Transport Zone**. If you select a Universal Transport Zone, this will create a universal logical switch. In this example, I selected a Transport Zone that is local to my vCenter.

8. By default, the logical switch inherits the control plane replication mode set in the Transport Zone. You can change this by selecting one of the available modes. For a universal logical switch, ensure that your multicast addresses do not conflict with any other multicast addresses across any NSX Manager in the environment.

9. IP discovery is enabled by default and allows **Address Resolution Protocol (ARP)** suppression between VMs connected to the same logical switch. There should not be any reason to disable this (optional).

10. Enable MAC learning setting if your virtual machines are having multiple MAC addresses or using virtual NICs that are trunking VLANs. This setting builds a VLAN/MAC pairing table on each vNIC.

You have now created your logical switch:

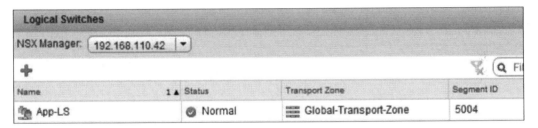

Now that we have created our logical switch, let's add some virtual machines to this switch.

Adding virtual machines to this switch will allow them to communicate with other instances that are a part of the logical switch, similar to how traditional networking works. You can connect virtual machines to a logical switch or to a Universal logical switch.

Let's add some virtual machines by performing the following set of steps:

1. Select the logical switch that you have created:

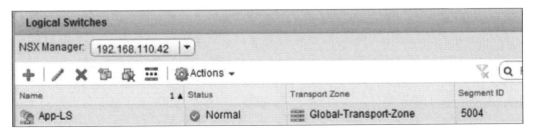

2. Click on the 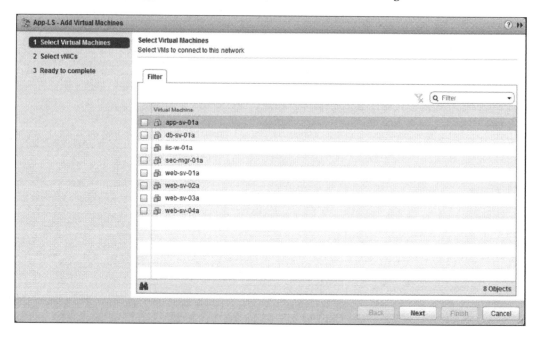 icon to add virtual machines to this logical switch:

3. Select the virtual machines from the list and click on **Next**. Notice that your virtual machines managed by the vCenter are listed here. For a multi-vCenter environment, you need to add virtual machines from each vCenter by selecting the appropriate NSX Manager.

4. Select the vNIC for the virtual machine that needs to be part of the logical switch network. You may have a scenario where a virtual machine has more than one vNIC that is part of multiple logical switches. Click on **Next** when done and click **Finish:**

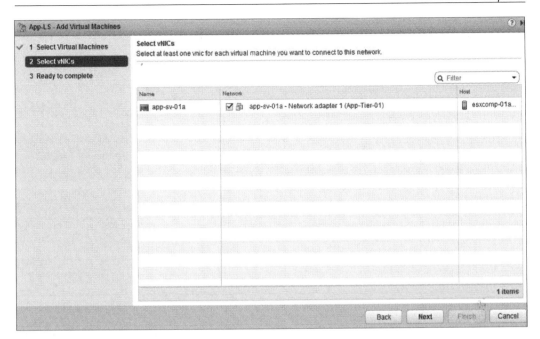

You have now connected a virtual machine to this logical switch. You can also associate a virtual machine to a logical switch by simply editing its settings and changing its vNIC association in vCenter.

You can review all the virtual machines connected to a logical switch by double-clicking the logical switch.

Go back to the logical switches view and double-click the logical switch we created. You will see the logical switch overview. In the following screenshot, you will notice that the **Virtual Machines** count is **1**. The number of hosts on which this logical switch is configured on is also listed.

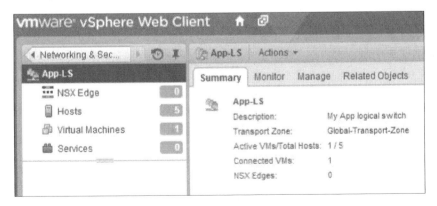

L2 bridges

A logical switch can be connected to a physical switch VLAN by means of an L2 bridge. This allows you to extend your virtual logical networks to access existing physical networks by bridging the logical VXLAN with the physical VLAN. This L2 bridging is accomplished by means of an NSX Edge logical router that maps to a single physical VLAN on the physical network. However, L2 bridges should not be used to connect two different physical VLANs or two different logical switches. Also, you cannot use a universal logical router to configure bridging, and a bridge cannot be added to a universal logical switch. This means, for a multi-vCenter NSX environment, you cannot extend a logical switch to a physical VLAN that is at another datacenter by means of L2 bridging.

Please note: L2 bridges should not be used to connect two different physical VLANs or two different logical switches.

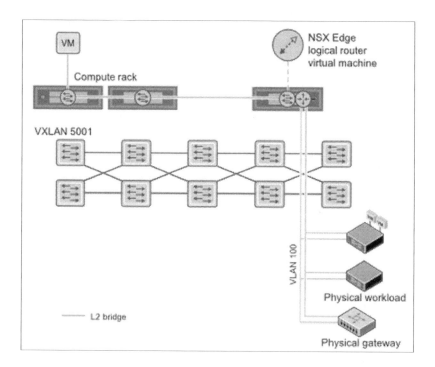

If **high availability (HA)** is configured for the NSX Edge router, the host on which the secondary edge appliance is present must also be connected to the physical VLAN to allow for a seamless bridge failover during a primary edge failure event.

To add an L2 bridge, an NSX Edge logical router must be deployed.

Deploying an NSX Edge logical router

To deploy an NSX Edge logical router, let's perform the following set of steps:

1. Go to **Home | Networking & Security | NSX Edges**.

2. Select the appropriate NSX Manager and click the **+** icon.

3. Select **Logical (Distributed) Router**. You cannot use **Universal Logical (Distributed) Router** to configure bridging:

4. Check **Enable High Availability** to ensure uptime during a downtime scenario. Ensure the other hosts participating in NSX Edge HA have physical VLAN connectivity to allow L2 bridging. Click **Next**.

5. Enter the admin password and set the logging level. Click **Next**.

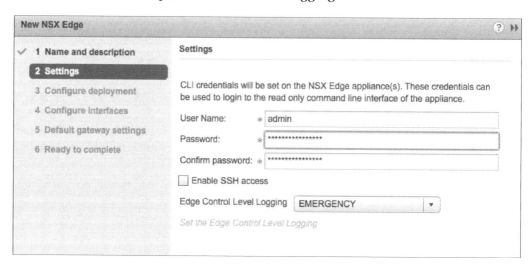

6. Select the datacenter and click the + icon to specify the resource pool and the datastore on which this appliance needs to be deployed:

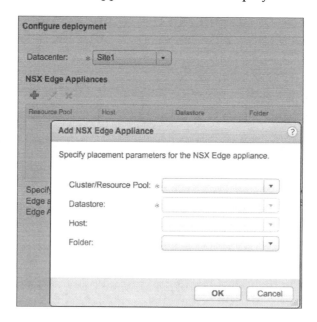

7. Next, we configure the HA interface configuration and the uplink interface for the NSX Edge. The uplink interface should be connected to a physical VLAN backed distributed port group to allow L2 bridging. Alternatively, it can be also connected to an edge gateway to route traffic for any north-south communication:

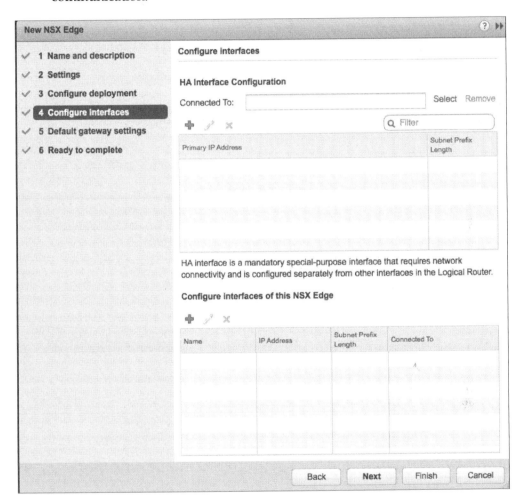

8. Configure the default gateway. Select the uplink for the edge and enter the gateway IP for your network. Click on **Next**.

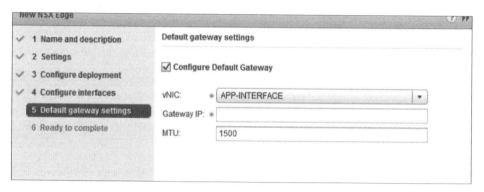

9. Review the summary and click **Finish**.

10. Monitor the progress in the tasks pane:

Now that the NSX Edge distributed logical router is deployed, let's configure this edge logical router, and enable the L2 bridging functionality:

1. Select NSX Edge **Logical Router** and double-click on it.

2. Go to the **Manage** tab, click on the **Bridging** tab, and then click on the + icon:

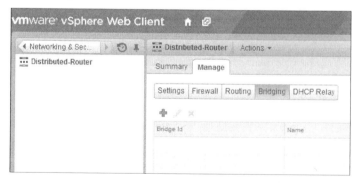

3. Name the bridge and select the logical switch and the distributed port group to enable L2 bridging between them. Click on **OK**:

4. Click **Publish changes**. Your L2 bridge is now set up:

The Edge services gateway

In the previous section, we looked at how to deploy an NSX Edge distributed logical router. Let's look at adding an NSX **Edge Services Gateway** (**ESG**). You can always deploy multiple NSX ESG virtual appliances. Each appliance is configured with interfaces and an edge appliance can have up to 10 virtual interfaces (uplink and internal). The internal interfaces act as gateways to all virtual machines in a port group, while the uplink interfaces can be connected to the outgoing network that can be your physical network.

Only the Enterprise administrator role that allows NSX operations and security management can deploy an ESG.

1. Go to **Home | Networking & Security | NSX Edges** and click on the **+** icon.

2. Select **Edge Services Gateway** and enter a unique name for the appliance. The ESG will be deployed in high availability mode if **Enable HA** is selected. Click on **Next**:

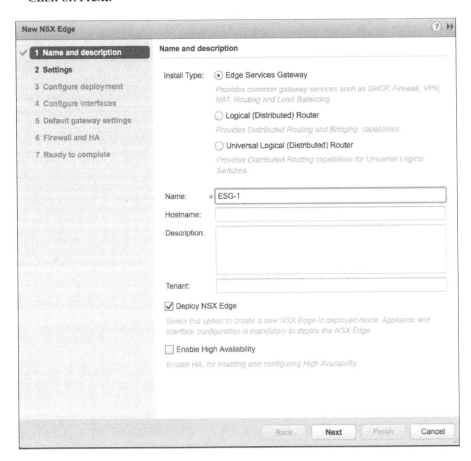

3. Enter the desired admin password. Enabling SSH access is optional and only recommended for troubleshooting purposes. Auto rule generation is enabled by default and allows the automatic creation of firewall rules, NAT, and the routing configuration that allows to control traffic for some Edge services. Disabling this will cause you to manually add these rules and configurations. Click on **Next**.

4. Select the appliance size depending on the size of your environment. You can also upgrade the appliance size after its deployment by simply using the **Convert to** option.

   As shown in the following screenshot, assign the appliance size value to a resource pool or a cluster and to a datastore. Click on **Next**.

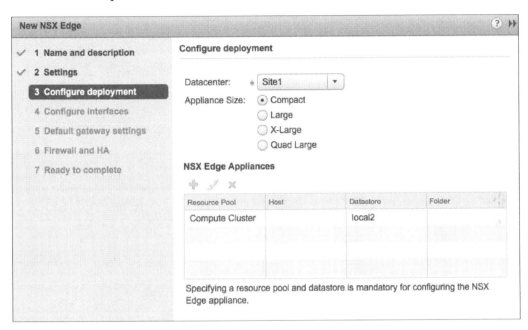

5. Click on **+** to configure interfaces to this Edge appliance. An Edge appliance must have at least one internal interface if it is configured for HA to work. An interface can be configured with both IPv4 and IPv6 addresses and can have multiple non-overlapping subnets. If an interface has more than one IP address, you can select the primary IP address. Only one primary IP address is allowed per interface, and the Edge uses this IP address as the source address for the locally-generated traffic. Optionally, you can specify the MAC address for each IP address you enter. You can also set the MTU, if needed. You can enable proxy ARP if you want the Edge gateway to answer ARP requests intended for virtual machines. Enabling the ICMP redirect option conveys the routing information to hosts.

6. When reverse path filtering is enabled, the reachability of the source address is verified in the packets being forwarded. In this mode, the packet must be received on the interface that the router would use to forward the return packet. It is enabled by default. In loose mode, the source address must appear in the routing table.

7. Configure fence parameters if you want to reuse the IP and MAC addresses across different fenced environments. Click on **OK**:

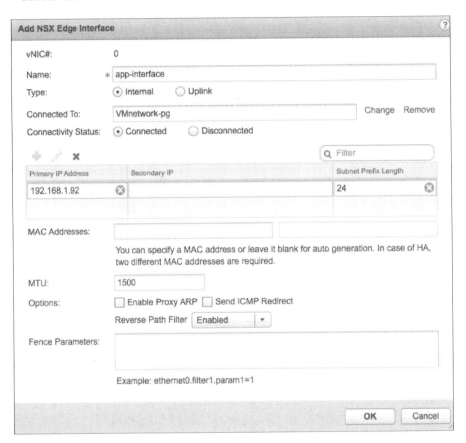

8. Click on **Next** to enter the default gateway IP information. After entering this information, click on **Next** again.

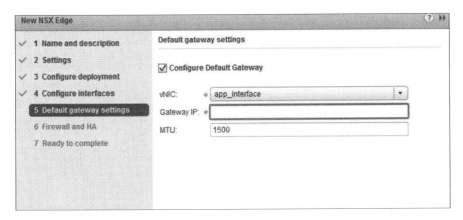

9. Select **Configure Firewall default policy** as seen in the following screenshot to change it to allow traffic that is legitimate. By default, the firewall will **deny all traffic**. You can enable logging, and logs are stored in the Edge appliance. If HA is enabled, it automatically chooses an internal interface and assigns **link-local IP addresses** to the Edge appliance. You can also set the HA heartbeat timeout as well, which determines the time interval after which a failure of the Edge appliance is declared and HA action is initiated. Click on **Next**.

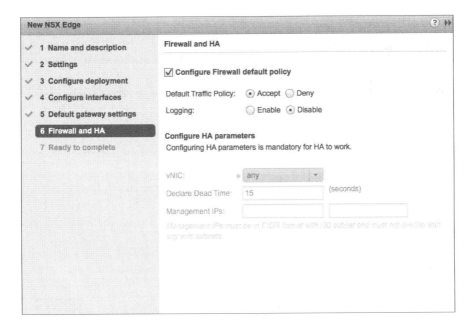

10. Click **Finish,** and you will see an Edge appliance being deployed:

We will look at how to configure Edge appliances in more detail in the upcoming sections and chapters.

The logical firewall

Logical firewalls are of two types—Distributed firewall and Edge firewall. The Distributed firewall is ideally deployed to protect east-west traffic, while the Edge firewall protects north-south traffic.

The firewall subsection interface allows you to add sections to separate firewall rules. Both L2 and L3 rules can have multiple sections that can be managed accordingly. For cross-vCenter environments, you must create a Universal section before you can add the universal rules, and you must manage the universal rules from the primary NSX Manager.

To add a firewall subsection, follow these steps:

1. Go to **Networking & Security | Firewall**.
2. Ensure that you have selected the right NSX Manager where you want to configure the rules. In a cross-vCenter environment, select the primary NSX Manager to add universal firewall rules:

3. The **General** tab allows you to add L3 rules, while the Ethernet tab allows you to add L2 rules.

4. Right-click on **Default Section Layer3** to add a new section. You can even scroll to the right to find the 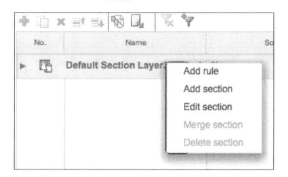 icon to add a new section:

5. Name the section appropriately. When **Mark this section for Universal synchronization** is enabled, it automatically marks this section as a Universal section. You will only see this option when configuring rules on the primary NSX Manager. Leaving this unchecked will apply this section only to the local domain. Click on **OK** when complete:

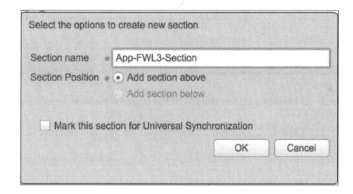

6. Click on **Publish changes**.

Now that the firewall section has been created, let's go ahead and add some rules to it. Firewall rules are applied to multiple objects at the source and destination levels for each rule. There are many vCenter objects that the rules can be applied to and a few of them are clusters, virtual machines, vNIC, and IP addresses as well. Before we go ahead to configure some local firewall rules, make sure your virtual machines have VMware tools installed on them.

The following steps are used to add local firewall rules:

1. Go to **Networking & Security | Firewall**.

2. Remember that the **General** tab allows you to add L3 rules, while the **Ethernet** tab allows you to configure L2 rules.

3. Click the **+** icon in the section where you want to add a new rule:

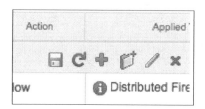

4. A new rule shows up with any under the section:

5. If you have multiple rules in a section and want to reorder the rules, highlight the rule and click the up or the down arrow icons to reorder the rule. The first matched rule is enforced in the firewall, so ordering your rules is important:

 Ordering rules is important as the first matched rule is enforced in the firewall.

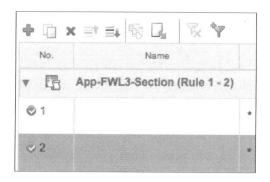

6. Point to the rule and click on the  icon to name the rule:

    Rule Name

    App-port443-rule

    OK   Cancel

7. Point to the source section and you will see two icons. Click 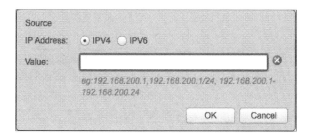 to specify an IP address as a source and the icon to specify an object. You can specify both IPv4 and IPv6 addresses. You can have a rule with both the IP address and the object together.

8. Click on the IP icon to add an IP address:

    Source

    IP Address: ⊙ IPV4 ○ IPV6

    Value:

    eg:192.168.200.1,192.168.200.1/24, 192.168.200.1-
    192.168.200.24

    OK   Cancel

9. To add an object, click on the icon:

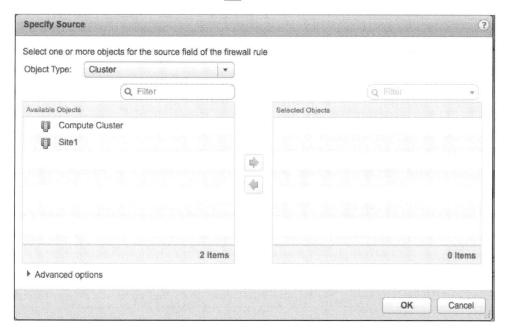

Specify Source

Select one or more objects for the source field of the firewall rule

Object Type: Cluster

Q Filter   Q Filter

Available Objects   Selected Objects

🗊 Compute Cluster

🗊 Site1

2 items   0 items

▸ Advanced options

OK   Cancel

10. Select the appropriate object from the **Object Type** dropdown. Select the available objects and click the arrow to include them. Click on **OK** when done:

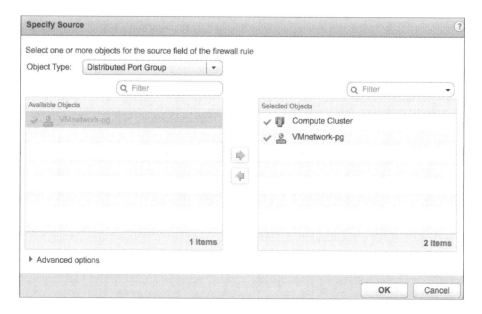

11. The **Advanced options** tab has a **Negate Source** option. By default, it's unchecked, and if checked, the rule will apply to all source traffic except the ones you have selected here. If unchecked, the rule will apply to all the traffic coming from the source set in the rule.

12. Similar to the source section, point to the destination section and you will see two icons. Click on ⬛ to specify an IP address as a source and the 🖊 icon to specify an object. You can specify both IPv4 and IPv6 addresses. You can have a rule with both the IP address and the object together. The advanced option in the destination has the **Negate destination** rule, which when selected will apply the rule to the traffic going to all the destinations except the listed destination.

13. Point to the service section to specify the kind of service to which you want the rule to allow traffic. Click on the ⬛ icon to define your port or the 🖊 icon to select from one of the predefined services. You can have both the port and the service in a rule.

14. Click on the ⬜ icon to define the service and click on **OK**:

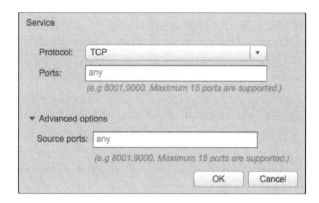

15. Click on the ✏️ icon to define a service or a service group:

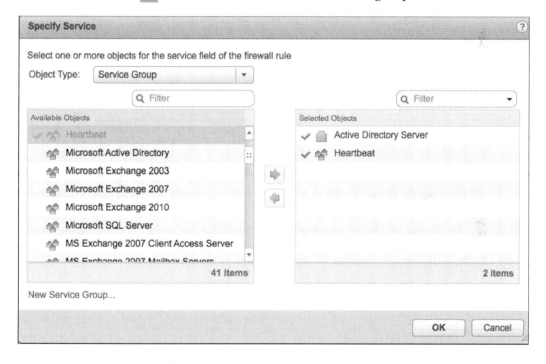

You can also click on **New Service Group** and define your own service group. Once defined, this group is automatically added to the list of service groups. Click on **OK**.

16. Go to the actions section to define the rule's behavior. Click on the Edit icon to define the action:

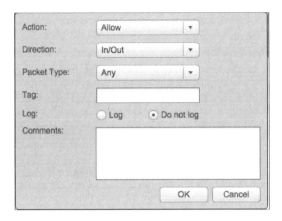

17. The **Applied to** section identifies the scope in which the rule is applicable. Click on the Edit icon to define the scope. You can select specific Edge gateways or all the Edge gateways to which this rule will apply. Click on **OK**:

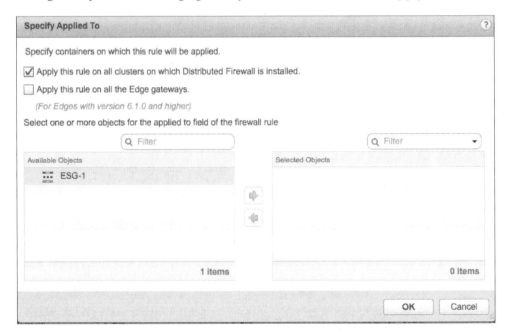

18. When done, click **Publish changes** and the rule will be published.

In a cross-vCenter NSX environment, rules created in the Universal Firewall section are replicated to the secondary NSX Managers. To create a Universal Firewall rule, follow these steps:

1. A universal firewall section is represented by the ![icon] icon. Click on the + sign in the section to add a universal rule.

2. Follow the preceding procedure to add a rule and click **Publish changes** when done.

To delete a firewall rule, simply select the rule by clicking on it and then click on the ![X] icon to delete the rule. Once done, you have to publish the changes for the deletion to take effect.

You can exclude certain virtual machines from being protected by the Distributed firewall. The NSX Manager, NSX controllers, and Edge appliances are automatically excluded. VMware recommends that the **service exclusion list** should contain the vCenter server, a SQL server for vCenter, and any virtual machines that are running in promiscuous mode. To add virtual machines to the exclusion list, follow these steps:

1. Go to **Networking & Security | NSX Managers | Manage | Exclusion List**.

2. Click the + icon and select the virtual machine to add to the exclusion list as seen in the following screenshot:

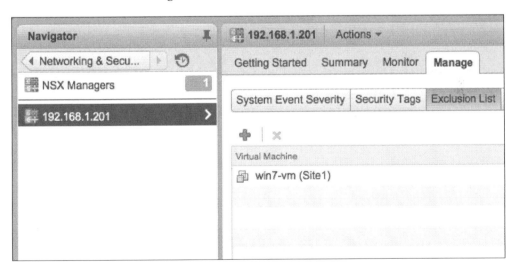

3. Click on **OK** when done. The virtual machine is no longer protected by the Distributed firewall.

The NSX ESG also allows a firewall protection that protects the north-south traffic in your environment. Let's look at how to configure the Edge firewall. The default Edge firewall policy blocks all the traffic. To access the Edge firewall, you must have an Edge gateway services appliance deployed and configured:

1. Go to **Networking & Security | NSX Edges** and double-click on the Edge appliance listed.

2. Click on the **Manage** tab and go to **Firewall:**

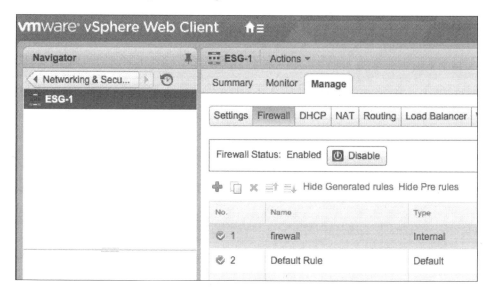

3. You should see the rules that include a default rule.

4. You can change the rule's behavior by pointing to the **Action** row and by editing it to a new action that you prefer.

The process to add a new rule is similar to the logical firewall described previously. You can click on the + icon and continue to name the rule. Any new rules added are marked as user type. Once you configure your rule, click **Publish** to publish and apply the rule. You can also change the order/priority of the rule by clicking on the Up or Down arrows.

 The Edge Services Gateway firewall is ideally suited to protect north-south traffic, while the Distributed Logical firewall protects the east-west traffic.

Summary

We began this chapter by discussing and deploying primary and secondary NSX Managers followed by deploying Transport Zones that define the scope of your logical switch in your environment. A logical switch can only be part of one Transport Zone, and there can only be one Universal Transport Zone in a cross-vCenter NSX environment. We then looked at how to create logical switches and L2 bridges. L2 bridges connect your logical networks to your physical networks for seamless network integration and extension. We looked at how to deploy a distributed logical router to enable L2 bridging. We also got started with the **Edge Services Gateway (ESG)** by deploying it. We protected our environment by deploying the logical firewall and configuring rules in it. We finished the chapter by configuring the ESG firewall service, which is similar to the logical firewall configuration. Ideally, the ESG firewall protects north-south traffic, while the logical firewall protects the east-west traffic.

In the next chapter, we will look at the NSX Edge gateway services and deploy and configure multiple Edge services.

5
Edge Services Gateway

We were introduced to the NSX **Edge services gateway** (ESG) in the previous chapter. We will continue to explore the deployment and configuration of different services that an ESG has to offer. We will look at configuring **OSPF and BGP routing** using the ESG. We will then walk through the deployment of logical Edge load balancers. ESG also offers the ability to set up virtual private networks that enable secure access to your environment. We will look at how to configure virtual private networks followed by the configuration of DNS and DHCP services. We will finish the chapter by looking at some more ESG configurations.

In this chapter, we will cover the following topics:

- DNS and DHCP services
- Routing
- Logical Edge Load balancers
- Virtual Private Networks
- More Edge services and configurations

DNS and DHCP services

NSX ESG offers DNS and DHCP services. Let's look at how to configure these services in the NSX Edge gateway.

DHCP service

NSX allows one-to-one static NAT IP address allocation and IP address pooling. When the DHCP service is set up, it listens to all the DHCP discovery requests on the internal interfaces and responds.

1. Go to **Home | Networking & Security | NSX Edges**, double-click on NSX Edge, and go to **Manage | DHCP**:

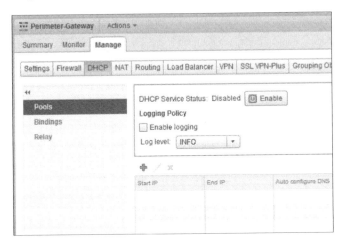

2. Click the **+** icon to add a new pool:

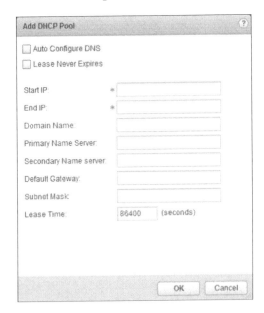

3. Enabling **Auto Configure DNS** allows you to use configure DNS automatically for every DHCP binding.

4. Enabling **Lease Never Expires** binds the IP address to the MAC address forever.

5. Enter **Start IP** and **End IP**. Fill in the rest of the form with applicable values and click on **OK** when done.

6. Now that a pool has been added, let's go ahead and enable the DHCP service.

7. Click on **Enable** and click on **Publish Changes**. You can also enable logging by selecting **Enable Logging** and setting the appropriate log level.

DNS service

NSX Edge can be configured with external DNS servers and can relay name resolution requests.

1. Go to **Home** | **Networking & Security** | **NSX Edges**, double click on **Edge**, and then go to **Manage** | **Settings** | **Configuration**:

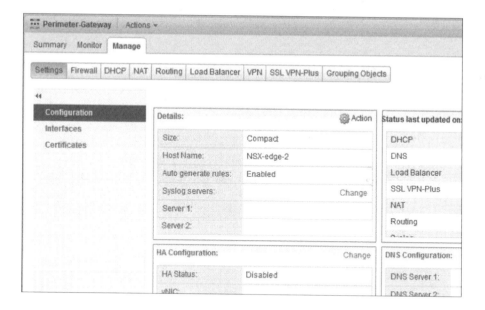

2. In the **DNS Configuration** section, click **Change:**

3. Select **Enable DNS service** to enable the service. Enter the external DNS server names and the cache size, if required. Select **Enable Logging** if needed, and click on **OK** when done.

Routing

In the previous chapter, we looked at how to deploy a logical router and NSX ESG. We will now look at how to enable routing services using the NSX ESG. These services allow more customized routing within your environment to suit your needs. You can configure the default gateway for the router and **ECMP (Equal Cost Multi-Path Routing)** that allows a **highly available deployment of multiple Edge gateways** to prevent bottlenecks. You can even configure a dynamic routing that updates routing tables with real-time logical network changes. All these can be set by editing the global configuration of an ESG.

Once the ESG is deployed, follow these steps for a global configuration:

1. Go to **Home | Networking & Configuration | NSX Edges**.

2. Double-click the Edge device that needs to be configured.

3. Go to **Manage | Routing | Global Configuration**:

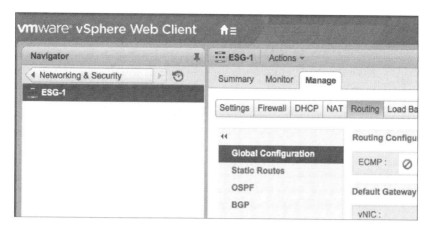

4. To enable ECMP, click on **Enable**. ECMP allows the next-hop packet to be forwarded to a single destination over multiple best paths that can be added statically or dynamically using routing protocols such as OSPF and BGP. These multiple paths are added as comma-separated values when defining the static routes.

5. To add a default gateway, click on **Edit** under the **Default Gateway** section.

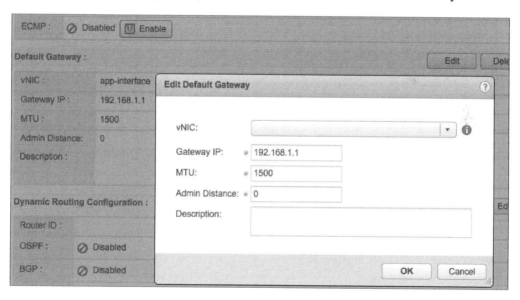

6. Select an interface that will be the outgoing interface for the next hop.

7. Set **Gateway IP**.

8. **Admin Distance** is a metric used to choose which route to take when multiple routes are available for a network. The lower the metric, the higher the priority. The value ranges from 1 to 255. Default ranges—Connected (**0**), Static (**1**), External BGP (**20**), OSPF Intra-Area (**30**), OSPF Inter-Area (**110**), and Internal BGP (**200**). Click on **OK**.

To configure dynamic routing, follow these steps:

1. Click **Edit** in the dynamic routing configuration section.

2. Router ID shows the first uplink of the Edge appliance that is used to push the routes to the kernel for dynamic routing.

3. Select **Enable Logging** to enable the logs.

4. Click on **Publish Changes** to save your settings.

To set a static route in the Edge gateway, do the following:

1. Go to **Home | Networking & Services | NSX Edges**, double-click on the Edge appliance, and then navigate to **Manage | Routing**.

2. Select **Static Routes** on the left-hand side menu:

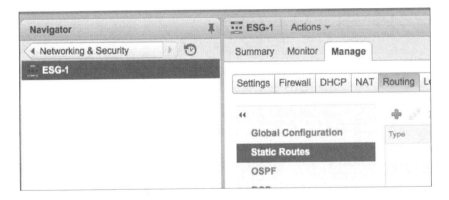

3. Click the **+** icon and you will see the following screenshot:

4. Enter a network under **Network** using the CIDR notation. For example, `192.168.1.0/24`.

5. Enter the **Next Hop** information. This is an IP address that the Edge is able to reach directly. If ECMP is configured, then multiple next-hop IP addresses can be mentioned with a comma.

6. Select an interface on which this static route will apply.

7. Select the appropriate **Admin Distance.**

8. Click on **OK.**

9. Click **Publish Changes** when done.

Configuring Edge Services Gateway OSPF

The ESG supports the OSPF, BGP, and IS-IS routing protocols. An ESG can learn and advertise routes when configured with the OSPF routing protocol. When there are routes of equal cost, OSPF provides dynamic load balancing between these routes. Routing table sizes becomes a challenge, and an OSPF network limits the size of these routing tables by dividing the network into routing areas to optimize traffic flow. An area is identified by an area ID and comprises routers, links, and a logical collection of OSPF networks that have the same area identification.

Open Shortest Path First (OSPF) is a routing protocol that uses a link state routing algorithm and operates within a single autonomous system.

Before we begin, we will ensure that a Router ID is configured. As we covered earlier, a Router ID is simply an uplink interface for the ESG that connects to the external peer. Perform the following set of steps to configure a Router ID:

1. Log in to NSX and navigate to **Home | Networking & Security | NSX Edges**, double-click on the ESG, and then go to **Manage | Routing | OSPF**:

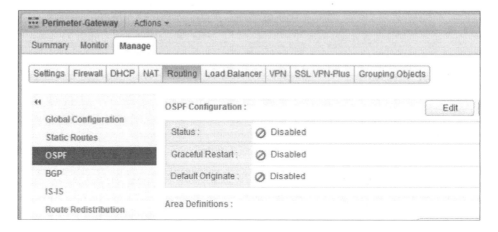

2. Click **Edit** to enable the **OSPF** configuration:

3. Click **Enable OSPF**. And, **Enable Graceful Restart** allows non-stop packet forwarding even if the OSPF process is being restarted. This helps in non-disruptive packet routing.

4. If you want your ESG to advertise itself as a default gateway to its peers, select **Enable Default Originate**. Then, click on **OK** when done.

5. We need to configure the OSPF areas. By default, **Area 51** is configured, which can be deleted if needed.

6. Click the **+** icon to add a new area:

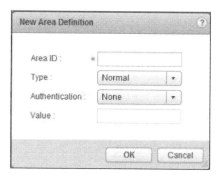

7. Type in an **Area ID**—it can be an IP address or a decimal number. If your area contains a specific network segment, you could type in 192.168.1.0 to easily identify that area. Next, select the type of area—**Normal** or **NSSA**. **NSSA** stands for **Not-So-Stubby Area**. NSSA prevents the flooding of external autonomous system link state advertisements by relying on the default routes to external destinations. Typically, NSSAs are placed at the Edge of an OSPF routing domain.

8. Next, select the type of **Authentication**. This is optional but, once set, you need to ensure that all the routers that are a part of the area have the same authentication type set with the same password. For MD5 authentication, both receiving and transmitting routers must have the same key configured. Click on **OK** when done.

9. Now that we have an area defined, we will proceed to map an interface to that area. In **Area to Interface Mapping,** click on the **+** icon:

10. Select the interface and the area ID to map. There are optional advanced settings that can be changed. **Hello Interval** is the default interval between the hello packets sent to the interface. **Dead Interval** is the timeout interval before the router declares a neighbor down. **Priority** is the default routing priority for the interface. Finally, the cost of the interface displays the default overhead required to send packets over that interface. You can define the cost based on the bandwidth of an interface so that the Edge can determine what the lowest cost to route traffic is across multiple interfaces. The higher the bandwidth of an interface, the lower the cost.

11. Click on **OK** when done.

12. Click on **Publish Changes** when done.

Configuring OSPF on a logical distributed router

Configuring OSPF on a logical distributed router enables VM connectivity across logical routers. Also, it forms a bridge between a logical router and the ESG. Configuring OSPF on a logical distributed router is similar in many ways to configuring OSPF on an ESG.

Ensure that a Router ID is configured. Perform the following set of steps:

1. Go to **Home** | **Networking & Security** | **NSX Edges**, double-click on your logical distributed router, and go to **Manage** | **Routing** | **OSPF**:

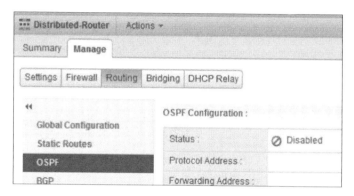

2. Click **Edit** under **OSPF Configuration:**

3. Click **Enable OSPF**. Under **Protocol Address**, enter the IP address that the OSPF protocol will use to form adjacencies with its peers. The forwarding address is then used by the distributed router (in the hypervisor) to forward packets. Click on **OK**.

4. Configuring the OSPF areas and **Area to Interface Mapping** is similar to the configuration described in the ESG.

5. Once done, click on **Publish Changes**.

Configuring BGP

Let's look at how to configure the border gateway protocol. BGP makes **core routing decisions** and includes a table of IP networks.

Border Gateway Protocol (BGP) is an exterior gateway protocol designed to exchange routing information among **Autonomous Systems (AS)** on the Internet. BGP is relevant to network administrators of large organizations that connect to two or more ISPs, as well as to Internet Service Providers who connect to other network providers. If you are the administrator of a small corporate network or an end user, then you probably don't need to know about BGP.

1. Go to **Home** | **Networking & Security** | **NSX Edges**, double-click on **NSX Edge**, and go to **Manage** | **Routing** | **BGP**:

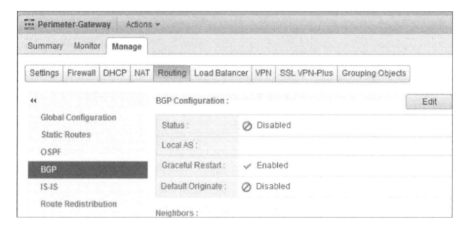

2. Click **Edit** under **BGP Configuration**.

3. Click on **Enable BGP**. Then, click on **Enable Graceful Restart** to continue to forward packets even if the BGP process restarts. The **Enabling Default Originate** option allows this Edge to advertise itself as a gateway to its peers. Type the Router ID in **Local AS** (Autonomous system). This is what the router uses to advertise itself to the routers in other autonomous systems.

4. In **Neighbors,** click the **+** icon:

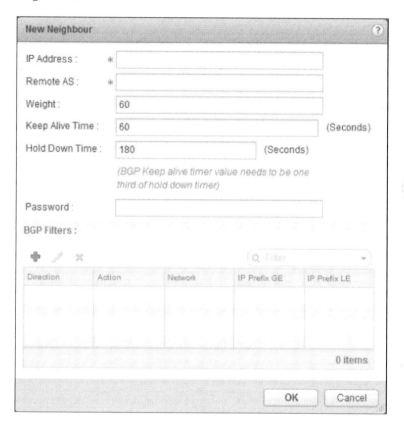

5. Type **IP Address** of the neighbor that is the peer of this router.

6. Next, type in a **Remote AS**. The **Weight** parameter determines the priority of the route.

7. **Keep alive time** determines how often keep alive messages are sent to peers. **Hold down timer** determines the timeout time before it declares a peer dead.

8. If authentication is required, set a password in the **Password** section but ensure that each of the BGP neighbors is configured with the same password.

9. To filter any routes, click on the + icon Under **BGP Filters**:

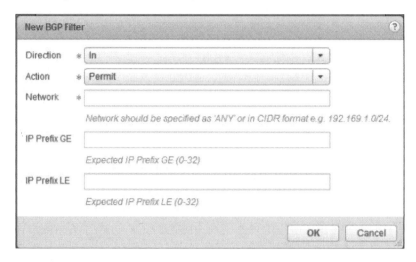

10. Set **Direction** to filter the traffic and the action to perform. Next, type the **Network** parameter (in the CIDR format) by which you want to filter traffic to or from the neighbor. Next, enter **IP Prefixes** and click on **OK**.

11. Click on **Publish Changes** when done.

Configuring the IS-IS protocol

IS-IS (Intermediate System to Intermediate System) is a link-state routing protocol that moves information by determining the best path in a packet switched network.

To set up the IS-IS protocol, follow these steps:

1. Go to **Home | Networking & Security | NSX Edges**, double-click on an Edge, and go to **Manage | Routing | IS-IS**:

2. Click on **Edit** and select **Enable IS-IS**. Type in **System Id** and select an **IS Type**. **Level 1** is intra, **Level 2** is inter area, and **Level 1-2** is both.

3. Type in **Domain Password** and **Area password**.

4. Next, define the IS-IS areas. Click on **Edit** in the **Areas** tab, enter three area IP addresses, and click on **Save**.

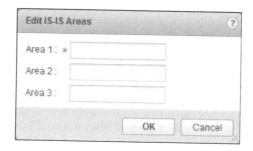

5. Click on **+** in the interface mapping.

6. Choose a value for the **Circuit Type** parameter that is the IS-IS type of Level 1, Level 2, or both.

7. **Hello interval** displays the frequency in milliseconds between the hello packets sent to the interface.

8. **Hello Multiplier** is the timeout for the IS-IS hello packets. **LSP Interval** is the time delay between successive IS-IS link state packets.

9. **Metric** is used to calculate the cost of sending traffic from each interface to other destinations.

10. **Priority** determines the priority of the interface and the highest priority interface becomes the designated router.

11. Next, type the number identifying the mesh group to which this interface belongs.

12. Then, type the authentication password for this interface and click on **OK**:

13. Click on **Publish Changes**.

Route redistribution configuration

In an environment where there are multiple routing protocols being used, route redistribution enables cross-protocol route sharing.

1. Go to **Home | Networking & Security | NSX Edges**, double-click on an NSX Edge, and go to **Manage | Routing | Route Redistribution**:

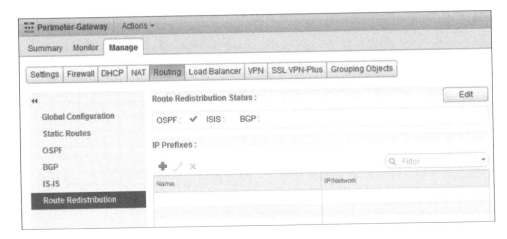

2. Click on **Edit** to select the protocols for which you want to enable route redistribution. Only configured protocols will show, as seen in the following screenshot:

3. Click the **+** icon to add an IP prefix:

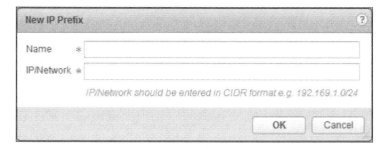

4. Next, you need to specify the redistribution criteria for the IP prefix entered. Click the **+** icon in the route redistribution table.

5. Select the appropriate **Prefix Name** value from the drop-down menu.

6. Next, specify the **Learner Protocol** value that will be used to learn routes from other protocols.

7. The **Allow learning from** parameter allows you to specify the protocols from which the routes will be learned.

8. Click on **OK** when done:

9. Click **Publish Changes** when done.

Logical Edge load balancers

Load balancers allow network traffic to be **balanced across multiple servers** to increase performance and also allow a high availability of services. This distribution of an incoming service among multiple servers is transparent to the end users, which makes the deployment of load balancers a critical component in any environment.

 A good use case for load balancers for further reading — http://cloudmaniac.net/load-balance-vmware-psc-with-nsx/.

ESG offers logical Edge load balancers that allow you to utilize the load balancing functionality and distribute incoming traffic across multiple virtual machine instances.

An ESG instance must be deployed in order to enable the load balancer service. There are multiple steps in configuring a load balancer service that begins with enabling the service, followed by configuring the application profile to define the behavior based on traffic type. Once these are defined, you will create a service monitor to enable a health check of the services behind the load balancer. This will allow you not to send traffic to a dead node. You then create a server pool that has the list of the servers participating in the load balancer and a virtual node that will receive all the traffic and distribute it among the pool based on the policies set.

To configure the load balancer service, do the following:

1. Go to **Home | Networking & Security | NSX Edges**, double-click on an Edge gateway, and go to **Manage | Load Balancer | Global Configuration**:

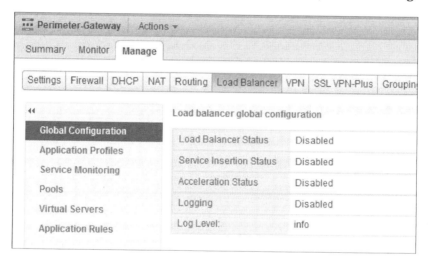

2. Click on **Edit** to enable the load balancer service. You should see something like the following screenshot:

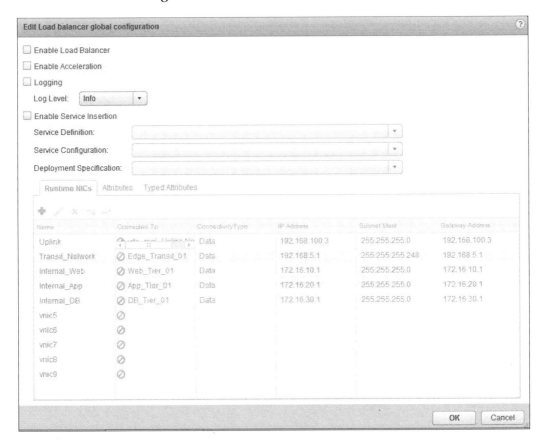

Select **Enable Load Balancer** to enable the load balancer service.

Enable Acceleration enables the Edge load balancer to use the faster L4 load balancer engine rather than the slower L7 engine.

The Layer4 load-balancer takes routing decisions based on IPs and TCP or UDP ports. It has a packet view of the traffic exchanged between the client and a server and takes decisions packet by packet. The layer 4 connection is established between a client and a server.

A layer 7 load balancer takes routing decisions based on IPs, TCP, or UDP ports, or any other information it can get from the application protocol (mainly HTTP). The layer 7 load balancer acts as a proxy and maintains two TCP connections: one with the client and another with the server.

Logging allows you to specify the level of logging. Increasing the logging level will cause a lot of data to be collected on the Edge appliance. In such instances, a syslog server is recommended as the best practice.

Enabling Service Insertion allows the Edge appliance to work with a third-party load balancer directly.

 A syslog server is recommended in order to capture all logs in the environment.

3. Click on **OK** to enable the load balancer service.

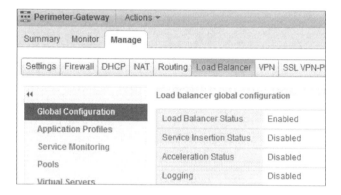

Now that the load balancer service is enabled, we will proceed to create a service monitor to define health check parameters. This service monitor is associated with a pool of servers that will be serving the traffic behind the load balancer. Perform the following set of steps to create a service monitor:

1. Go to **Home | Networking & Security | NSX Edges**, double-click on an Edge appliance, and then go to **Manage | Load Balancer | Service Monitoring**:

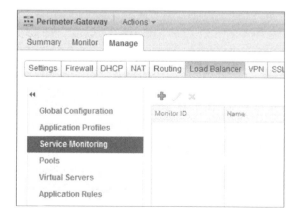

2. Click on the **+** icon to add a new service monitor:

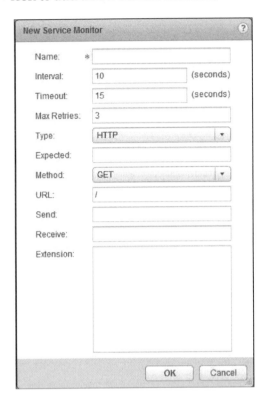

3. Enter a **Name** for the service, followed by the interval frequency to ping the service.

4. Enter a **Timeout** for the maximum time in seconds to receive a response, followed by the maximum allowed retries before declaring a failure.

5. **Type** defines the way in which the service is checked for the **HTTP** and **HTTPS** types.

6. Enter the expected string in the **Expected** section. This is what the monitor should expect when it checks for the HTTP or the HTTPS service.

7. Select a **Method** and the base URL to test. If the method is POST instead of GET, type the data in **Send** to send it to the server. When the **Expected** string matches the monitor, it will also match the **Receive** string.

8. **Extension** allows you to enter advanced monitoring parameters such as key:value pairs. This is optional.

9. Click on **OK** when done.

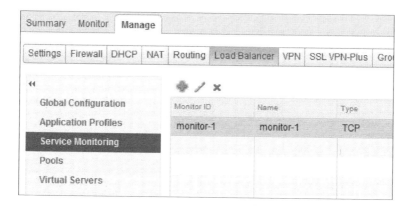

We will now proceed to create a server pool so that we can associate it with the service monitor.

1. Click on **Pools** in the **Load Balancer** section of the Edge appliance:

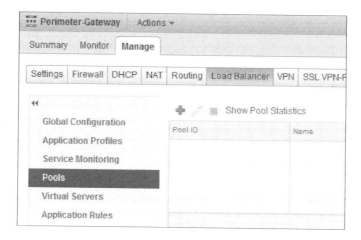

2. Click on the **+** icon to create a new pool:

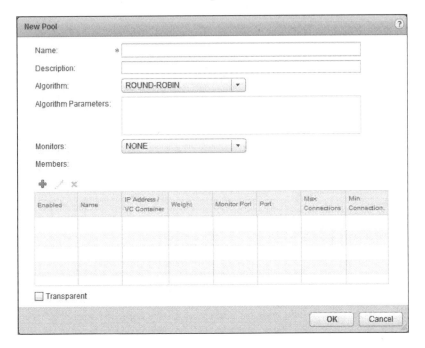

3. Enter the name of the pool. Select the appropriate algorithm for the service. This depends on what service you are working with to load-balance the traffic. The four options are as follows:

    ○ **ROUND-ROBIN**: In this, each server is used in turn according to the priority or weight assigned to it.

    ○ **IP_Hash**: This selects a server based on the hash of the source and destination IP addresses of each packet.

    ○ **Least_Conn**: This directs new connections to the server in the pool that has the least connections active.

    ○ **URI**: The URI is hashed and divided by the total weight of all the servers in the pool. The result is used to decide which server in the pool will take the request.

4. Select a value for **Monitors** that applies to the pool from the drop-down menu.

5. Add members to the pool by clicking on the **+** icon.

6. Type in a **Name** for the member followed by **IP address** or a virtual center object such as a cluster.

7. Type in the **Port** member where the traffic is to be sent. **Monitor Port** is the port where a member receives health check pings. **Weight** determines how much traffic this member can handle.

8. **Max Connections** and **Min Connections** allow you to manage traffic and the number of connections appropriately. Click on **OK**.

9. The **Transparent** option allows the backend servers in the pool to see the source IP of the request. Transparent is disabled by default and the backend servers only see the traffic coming in from the internal load balancer IP.

10. Click on **OK** when done.

Before we create a virtual server to map to the pool, we have to define an application profile that defines the behavior of a particular type of network traffic. When traffic is received, the virtual server processes the traffic based on the values defined in the profile. This allows greater control over the management of your network traffic.

1. Select **Application Profiles:**

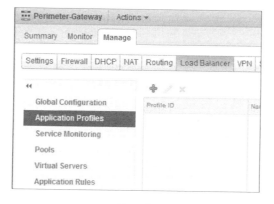

2. Click the + icon.

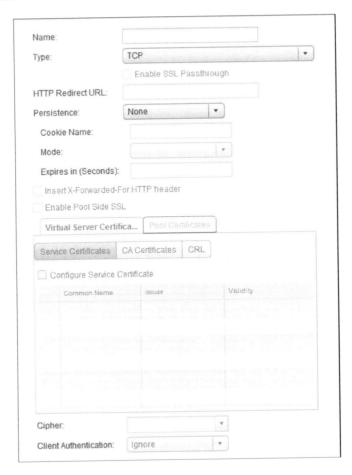

3. Type a **Name** for the profile and the type of traffic. If you want to redirect HTTP traffic, enter the URL to which it needs to be redirected.

4. Specify a **Persistence** that applies to the profile. Persistence tracks and stores any session data. There are different persistence methods supported for different types of traffic.

5. Selecting HTTPS allows you to have terminal SSL certificates in the load balancer, or even configure SSL to pass through your backend pool servers.

6. Select any Cipher algorithms that apply and are negotiated during the SSL/TLS handshake.

7. Click on **OK** when done.

Now that we have created the application profile, let's create a virtual server and associate it with the pool. Once this is done, external traffic can be directed to the virtual server IP that in turn distributes traffic across pool members based on the algorithm we have defined. Perform the following set of steps to create a virtual server and associate it with a pool:

1. Select **Virtual Servers** and click the **+** icon to add a new virtual server:

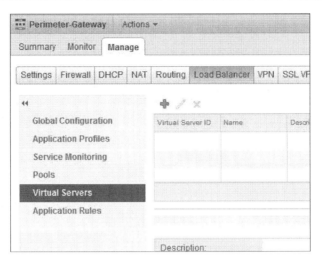

2. You will see the **New Virtual Server** dialog box:

3. Select an **Application Profile** for your virtual server.

4. Type a **Name** for the virtual server.

5. Enter the **IP address** of the virtual server. This is the IP address through which the load balancer will receive all external traffic.

6. Select the **Protocol** that the virtual server will handle and the port that will receive the traffic.

7. Select a **Default Pool** and set the connection limits, if applicable.

8. Click on **OK** when done.

Next, let's look at application rules to understand their application and configuration. An application rule allows you to specify the rules and logic to manage your traffic to make intelligent redirection. You can use an application rule to directly manipulate and manage IP application traffic. This becomes critical in fine-tuning your traffic to the application you are running behind the perimeter.

1. Log in to the vSphere web client and go to **Home | Networking & Security | NSX Edges**.

2. Double-click on an NSX Edge and navigate to **Manage | Load Balancer**:

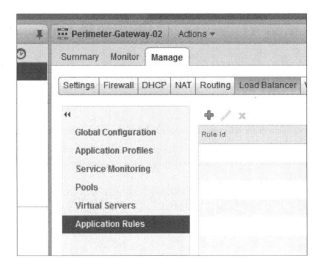

3. Click on **Application Rules** and click on the Add icon.

4. Type the name and a script for the rule.

 For more information, the application rule syntax can be referenced here—`http://cbonte.github.io/haproxy-dconv/configuration-1.5.html`.

5. Click on **OK** when done.

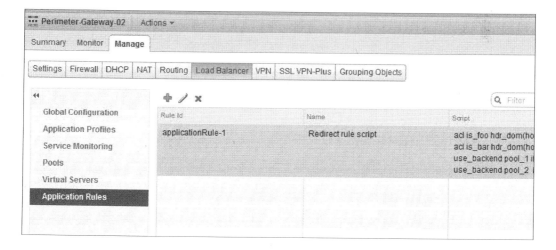

A good example of an application rule script is shown in the following. This script directs requests to a specific load balancer pool according to the domain name. The following rule directs requests to `foo.com` to `pool_1`, and to `bar.com` to `pool_2`:

```
aclis_foohdr_dom(host) -i foo
aclis_barhdr_dom(host) -i bar
use_backendpool_1 if is_foo
use_backendpool_2 if is_bar
```

You can also look into more rule syntax examples in VMware's NSX online documentation available at—`http://pubs.vmware.com/NSX-62/index.jsp?topic=%2Fcom.vmware.nsx.admin.doc%2FGUID-A5779D43-AC0F-4407-AF4A-0C1622394452.html`.

Virtual Private Networks

Virtual private networks (VPN) allow you to securely connect a remote device or a remote site to your corporate infrastructure. NSX Edge supports three types of VPN connectivity. SSL VPN-Plus allows remote users to access corporate applications securely. IP-SEC VPN offers a site-to-site connectivity, and L2 VPN allows you to extend your datacenter by allowing virtual networks to span across datacenters securely.

SSL VPN-Plus

SSL VPN-Plus allows remote users to securely access applications and servers in a private network. There are two modes in which SSL VPN-Plus can be configured—network access mode and web access mode.

In the network access mode, a remote user can access the internal private network securely. This is done by virtue of a VPN client that a remote user downloads and installs on their operating system. In web access mode, the remote user is able to access private networks without any VPN client software.

SSL VPN-Plus network access mode

Before we begin to configure the network access mode, make sure that the SSL VPN gateway is accessible externally over port 443. We will systematically configure the network access mode by following multiple steps:

1. Go to **Home** | **Networking & Security** | **NSX Edges**, double-click on the ESG device, and then navigate to **Manage** | **SSLVPN-Plus**:

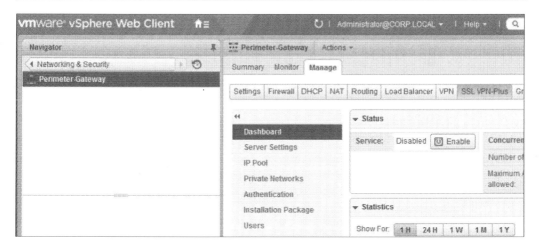

2. Click on **Server Settings** and then click on **Change** to select the IP address on which the server will respond.

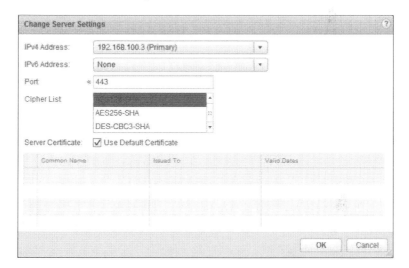

3. Select **IPv4 Address** or **IPv6 Address**, the desired **Port** number, and the encryption method. If you have a certificate installed, select that if needed.

4. Click on **OK** when done.

5. We will now continue to add an IP pool to provide an IP address to the remote user when a VPN connection is established.

6. On the **IP Pools** tab, click the **+** icon.

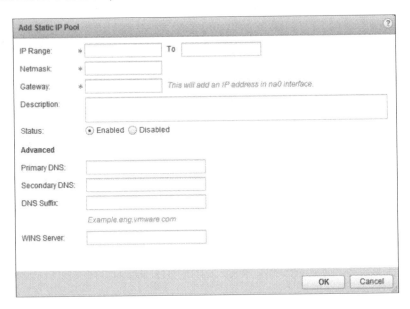

7. Type the **IP Range**, **Netmask**, and the **Gateway** values that are typically the external interface of the NSX Edge gateway.

8. Type in a **Description** for the pool followed by setting the status to **Enabled** to enable the pool. You may also add custom DNS settings and provide a WINS server if needed.

9. Click on **OK** when done.

10. We will now add the private network remote VPN users will be able to access. Click on the **Private network** tab on the left-hand side and click on the **+** icon.

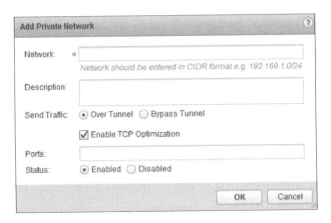

11. Enter a network in CIDR format and a description. Specify whether the traffic should traverse the tunnel or bypass the tunnel and be sent directly to the private server.

12. A tunnel here indicates that the SSL VPN-Plus has enabled the Edge gateway. If you choose to send traffic over the tunnel, leave **Enable TCP Optimization** checked to optimize the Internet speed followed by specifying the port numbers for which traffic will be optimized. The traffic for the ports that are not listed will not be optimized.

13. For multiple ports, you have to create multiple private networks that point to the same subnet with a different port each time.

14. Select **Enabled** for **Status**.

15. Click on **OK** when done.

16. We will now configure an authentication mechanism for users who will be able to access the VPN. ESG SSL VPN-Plus supports external authentication mechanisms such as Active Directory, LDAP, Radius, and RSA. Click on the **Authentication** tab and click on the + icon.

17. Select the appropriate **Authentication Server Type** and fill out the information. Wherever applicable, ensure that you enable SSL to encrypt all traffic.

18. The maximum **Timeout** value for VPN connection authentication is **3** minutes and is non-configurable.

We will now create an installation package for the end user. This installation package contains the VPN software client required to make the connection.

1. Click on the **Installation Package** tab and click the **+** icon.

2. Enter a **Profile Name** for the installation package. Type the FQDN or the external IP address for the ESG. This is the IP address that the client will connect to. If you need to bind additional Edge uplink interfaces, click on the **+** icon and add them.

3. Select the operating system for which the package needs to be created. By default, the package is created for Windows.

4. Select **Enabled** to advertise and display the installation package on the installation package page.

5. Customize the installation package by choosing your preferred parameter for Windows.

6. Click on **OK** when done.

7. Let's now add a remote user. Click on **Users** and click the + icon.

 Some useful LDAP configuration options are listed at the following URL:

http://vmw.re/1WcB1Fn

8. Fill in the form appropriately and click on **OK** when done.

9. Now that the setup is done, let's enable the SSL VPN-Plus service. Click on **Dashboard**, then click on **Enable**, and answer the prompt to enable the service. Once enabled, open a browser and access the ESG over HTTPS. Log in using the user name you created in Steps 7-8 to download the VPN client. Log in to the VPN client based on the user and authentication mechanism applicable.

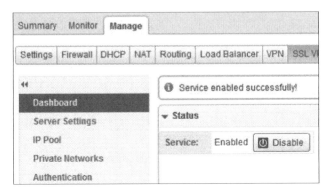

SSL VPN-Plus web access mode

In web access mode, a remote user can access internal networks securely without a VPN client. This is ideal for on-the-go systems or thin clients where deploying a VPN client is considered an unnecessary overhead. This is also an option to enable access to a specific web resource and not to an entire network.

We will first add a server that the remote user can connect to using their browser.

1. Go to **Home | Networking & Security | NSX Edges**, double-click on the ESG Edge, and navigate to **Manage | SSL VPN-Plus**.

2. Click on the **Web Resource** option.

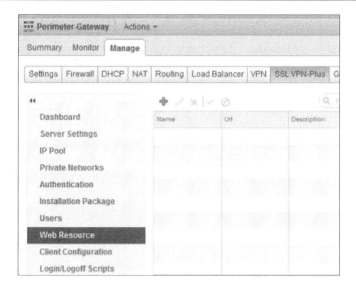

3. Click on the **+** icon to add a web resource.

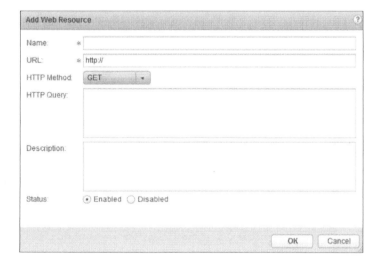

4. Enter the name and the URL of the resource you want remote users to access. Select the appropriate HTTP method and select **Enabled** to enable this web resource.

5. Click on **OK** when done.

6. Let's now add a remote user. Click on **Users** and click the + icon.

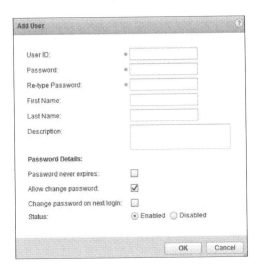

7. Fill in the form appropriately and click on **OK** when done.

8. We will now configure an authentication mechanism for users who will be able to access the VPN. The ESG, SSL VPN-Plus, supports external authentication mechanisms such as Active Directory, LDAP, Radius, and RSA. Click on the **Authentication** tab and click the + icon.

9. Select the appropriate **Authentication Server Type** and fill out the information. Wherever applicable, ensure that you enable SSL to encrypt all traffic.

10. The maximum **Timeout** value for a VPN connection authentication is **3** minutes and is nonconfigurable.

11. Click on **Server Settings** and then click on **Change** to select the IP address to which the server will respond.

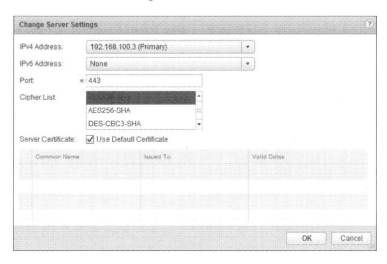

12. Select **IPv4 Address** or **IPv6 Address**, the desired port number and the encryption method. If you have a certificate installed, select that if needed. Click on OK when done.

13. Now that the setup is done, let's enable the SSL VPN-Plus service. Click on **Dashboard** and then click on **Enable**, and answer the prompt to enable the service. Once done, access the NSX Edge gateway's external IP address and log in to the web portal. You will now be redirected and will be able to access the web resource appropriately.

IPSEC VPN

The NSX Edge service gateway supports a site-to-site IPSEC VPN that allows you to connect a NSX ESG-backed network to another device at the remote site. A NSX Edge can establish secure tunnels with remote sites to allow secure traffic to flow between sites. The number of tunnels an Edge gateway can establish depends on the size of the Edge gateway deployed.

A compact Edge gateway can create a maximum of 512 tunnels. A large Edge gateway can create a maximum of 1,600 tunnels, while a quad-large can handle a maximum of 4,096 tunnels. An x-large Edge gateway can handle up to 6,000 tunnels.

NSX supports the AES (AES128-CBC), AES256 (AES256-CBC), Triple DES (3DES192-CBC), DH-2 (Diffie–Hellman group 2), DH-5 (Diffie–Hellman group 5), and AES-GCM (AES128-GCM) IPSEC VPN algorithms.

Before we begin to configure our IPSEC VPN, we need to ensure that dynamic routing is disabled on the Edge uplink to allow specific routes to be defined for any VPN traffic. Having dynamic routing enabled causes routes to be updated as the router learns about new routes that can cause traffic disruption in an IPSEC VPN setup.

Let's begin by first generating a certificate to enable certificate authentication. You can import a CA-signed certificate or use Open-SSL to generate a CA-signed certificate. Self-signed certificates cannot be used with IPSEC VPN. They can only be used with load balancers and SSL VPNs. Perform the following set of steps to generate a certificate to enable certificate authentication:

1. Go to **Home | Networking & Security | NSX Edges**, double-click on an Edge appliance, and navigate to **Manage | Settings | Certificates.**

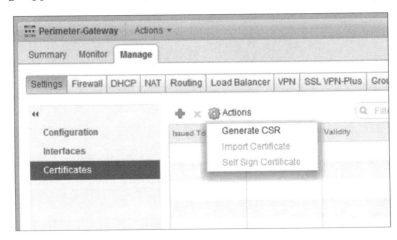

2. Click on **Actions** and then click on **Generate CSR**. This generates your CSR.

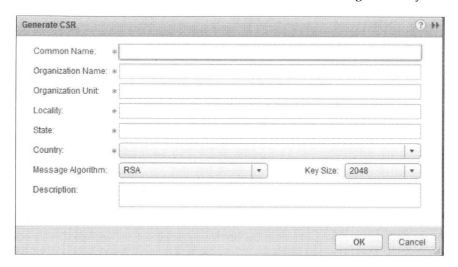

3. Fill out the appropriate details and click on **OK**.

4. We will now set **Global configuration status**. Click on the **VPN** tab and click on **IPsec VPN**:

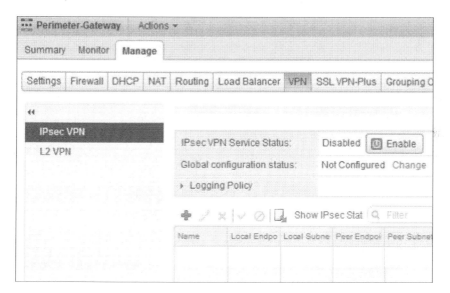

5. Click on **Change** next to **Global configuration status**.

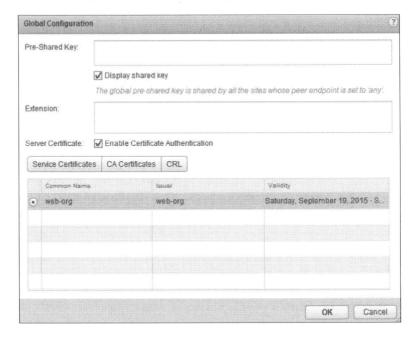

6. Enter the global preshared key that is shared by all the sites whose peer endpoints are set to **any**.

7. Select **Enable Certificate Authentication** and then select the appropriate certificate. Click on **OK** when done.

8. Next, we enable logging for our IPSEC VPN. Expand the logging policy and check **Enable Logging**. Set the appropriate logging level. Increasing the logging level increases the amount of data stored on the Edge appliance and can negatively impact performance.

 The best practice is to configure a syslog server so that all logs can be exported to it and not stored locally in the ESG appliance.

9. Next, we configure the IPSEC VPN parameters. Click the **+** icon.

10. Enter the name of the tunnel and enter the Edge gateway IP address in the **Local Id** field. This will be the peer ID on the remote site.

11. Type the IP address of the local endpoint, which is the IP address of your Edge gateway.

12. Next, type the local subnets that are shared between two sites.

13. Enter a **Peer Id** to uniquely identify the peer site. This ID must be the common name in the peer's certificate for any of the peers using the certificate authentication. Ideally, it is a good practice to stick to the IP address as the peer ID.

14. In **Peer Endpoint**, type the IP address of the peer site. Next, type the internal IP address of the peer subnet.

15. Now, select the appropriate encryption algorithm. If you require anonymous sites to connect to your VPN, enter the preshared key to allow such a capability. Clicking on **Display shared key** displays the key on the peer site.

16. Next, select the cryptography scheme that allows the NSX Edge and the peer site to establish a shared secret over an insecure channel.

17. In **Extension**, type one of the following:

    ° `securelocaltrafficbyip=IPAddress`: This redirects the Edge's local traffic through the IPSEC tunnel. This value is the default.

    ° `passthroughSubnets=PeerSubnetIPAddress`: This allows overlapping subnets on both sides.

18. Click on **OK** when done. The NSX Edge now creates a tunnel between the local subnet and the peer subnet.

19. Click on **Enable** and **Publish Changes** when done.

L2 VPN

L2 VPN allows you to stretch multiple logical networks across multiple sites. The networks can be both traditional VLANs and VXLANs. In such a deployment, a virtual machine can move between sites without any change in its IP address.

L2 VPN is deployed as a **client and a server,** where the destination Edge is the server and the source Edge is the client. Both the client and server learn the MAC addresses of both local and remote sites. For any site that is not backed by an NSX environment, a **standalone NSX Edge gateway** can be deployed.

Before we begin to configure L2VPN, ensure that a sub-interface is added to a trunk interface of the NSX Edge. You can learn more about adding a sub-interface in the Edge configuration section of this chapter.

To begin configuration for L2 VPN, follow these steps:

1. Go to **Home | Networking & Security | NSX Edges**, double-click the Edge appliance, and navigate to **Manage | VPN | L2 VPN**:

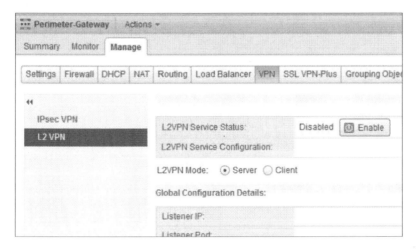

2. To configure the L2VPN server that is the destination Edge, select the **L2VPN Mode** to **Server** and click on the **Change** button:

3. In **Listener IP**, select the primary or the secondary IP of the Edge. Change the port if needed, and select the appropriate encryption algorithm.

4. Select the certificate, if configured, and click on **OK** when done.

5. Next, we add a peer site. Under **Site Configuration Details**, click the + icon.

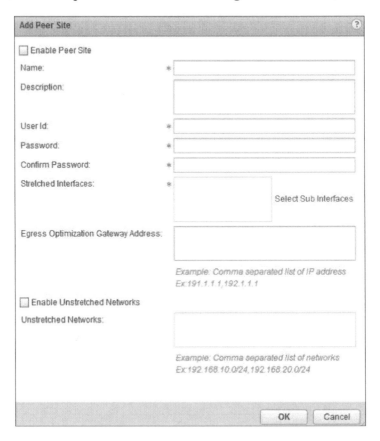

6. Enter a unique name for the peer site and a description, if necessary. Enter the username and password for the peer site for authentication.

7. Click on **Select Sub Interfaces** and select the appropriate interfaces. These are the interfaces that are stretched with the client.

8. If the default gateway for all the virtual machines is the same across both the sites, type in the gateway IP in the **Egress Optimization Gateway Address** section. This will allow local routing and increase performance.

9. By enabling **Enable Unstretched Networks**, you will be able to identify network subnets that you do not wish to extend between the two sites.

10. Make sure the **Enable Peer Site** option (at the top of the dialog) is checked and then click on **OK** when done.

11. Enter the **Server Address**, which is the L2VPN server IP or FQDN. Select the same encryption algorithm as set on the server and select the appropriate stretched interfaces.

12. Type in the **Egress Optimization Gateway Address**. Type the user credentials.

13. If the client NSX Edge does not have a direct internet connection, it can reach the server NSX Edge over a proxy server that can be set in the advanced settings.

14. Click on **OK** and then on **Publish Changes**.

15. Enable the L2VPN service on the client, which establishes the L2VPN connectivity between the sites.

More Edge services and configurations

In this section, we will look at a few configuration steps for some common actions that you will perform on the ESG. In a production environment, you will often perform these configurations either during initial setup or after.

We will be looking at adding a sub interface, forcing synchronization of NSX Edge with NSX Manager, configuring remote syslog servers, and redeploying an NSX Edge appliance.

Adding a sub interface

An NSX ESG can have up to ten internal, external (physical), or trunk interfaces, while an Edge distributed router can have up to eight uplink interfaces and up to a thousand internal (sub) interfaces.

A sub interface or an internal interface is a logical interface that is created and mapped to the physical interface. Sub-interfaces are simply a division of a physical interface into multiple logical interfaces. This logical interface uses the "parent" physical interface to move data. Remember that you cannot use sub-interfaces for HA because a heartbeat needs to traverse a physical port from one hypervisor to another between the Edge appliances.

To configure a sub-interface, do the following:

1. Go to **Home | Networking & Security | NSX Edges**, double-click an Edge appliance, and navigate to **Manage | Settings | Interfaces**:

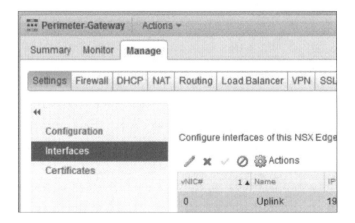

2. Click on the **Edit** icon to edit an interface.

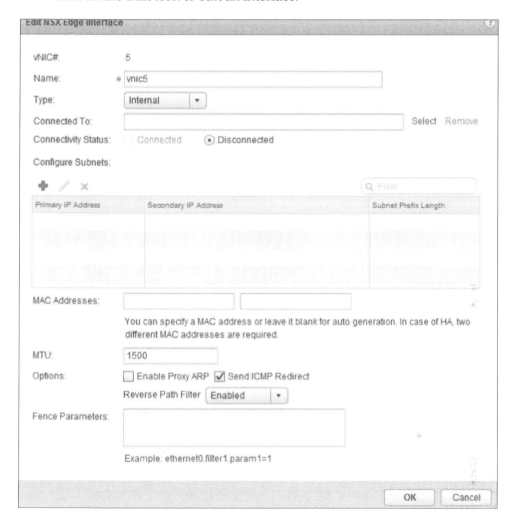

3. Enter a **Name** for the interface. Select **Trunk** from the **Type** drop-down menu.

4. Click on **Select** to select a port group to connect to this interface. Click the + sign to add a sub-interface to this trunk interface.

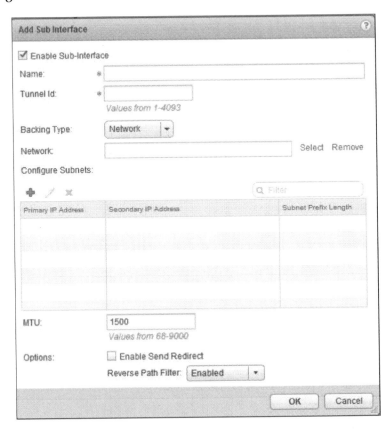

5. Enter the **Name** and **Tunnel Id** as applicable in your environment.

6. In **Backing Type**, select a VLAN for a VLAN network and type in the VLAN ID this sub-interface should use.

7. For **Network**, select a logical switch or a distributed port group so that NSX can use the VLAN ID for that switch or port group and use it in the trunk.

8. Selecting **None** creates an internal sub-interface that is used to route packets in a stretched network and an unstretched network.

9. Click on + to configure subnets. A sub-interface can have one primary IP and multiple secondary IPs. **Enable Send Redirect** allows you to convey routing information to hosts.

10. Click on **OK** to return to interface configuration.

11. Enter a MAC address. Sub-interfaces do not support HA, so you may leave this blank to allow auto generation.

12. Select the appropriate **MTU** value with a minimum of **1600**.

13. Click on **OK** when done.

Force-Syncing NSX Edge with NSX Manager

The NSX Manager holds all the configuration data for each NSX Edge and keeps a check of synchronization via regular polling between the NSX Manager and the ESG. A good example of an Edge appliance going out of sync is low disk space where additional new configuration data cannot be written to the appliance, causing it to go out of sync. Any ESG that is out of sync can be **resynchronized** by issuing a force sync request.

Force sync is a feature that synchronizes the Edge configuration of the NSX Manager with all of its components in an environment. A synchronization action is initiated from the NSX Manager to the NSX Edge that refreshes and reloads the Edge configuration. Initiating a force sync action causes minor north-south traffic interruption. The east-west traffic remains unaffected. The interruption is due to a reboot of the Edge appliances.

In a cross-vCenter environment, you have to first apply force sync on the NSX Edge at the primary NSX Manager site before applying it on the secondary sites.

To apply force sync, follow these steps:

1. Go to **Home | Networking & Security | NSX Edges**.

2. Select an Edge device, click on **Actions**, and select **Force Sync**.

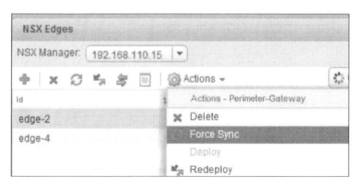

3. Click on **Yes** when the prompt appears to enforce the sync action.

Configuring remote syslog servers

VMware recommends configuring syslog servers to avoid log flooding on the Edge appliances. When logging is enabled, logs are stored locally on the Edge appliance and consume space. If left unchecked, this can have a performance impact on the Edge appliance and can also cause the Edge appliance to stop due to a lack of disk space. Perform the following set of steps to configure a remote syslog server:

1. Go to **Home | Networking & Security | NSX Edge**, double-click on an Edge appliance, and navigate to **Manage | Settings**.

2. Click on **Change** in the **Syslog servers** row.

3. Enter the Syslog server IP address and select the protocol as applicable. Click on **OK** when done.

Redeploying an NSX Edge

Occasionally, you will notice that your Edge appliance is not performing as expected. If force sync does not resolve this issue, then a redeploy is necessary. Redeploying an Edge appliance essentially redeploys the ESG and is a disruptive action.

In a multi-vCenter environment, you are required to first redeploy the NSX Edge appliance on the primary side before redeploying on the secondary side. It is necessary to redeploy both sides in a multi-vCenter environment.

1. Go to **Home** | **Networking & Security** | **NSX Edges**, select an Edge, and navigate to **Actions** | **Redeploy**:

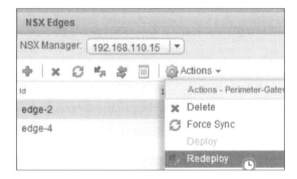

2. Click on **Yes** in the prompt to complete the redeploy process.

Summary

In this chapter, we looked at how to configure different supported routing protocols on the NSX Edge. We started the chapter and looked at the configuration of the DNS and DHCP services. Next, we looked at how to configure the OSPF, BGP, and IS-IS routing protocols. We also looked at the configuration of logical load balancers, which allow us to implement a load balancer for our applications. We then looked at the configuration of virtual private networks on our Edge appliance so that remote users can connect securely. Edge supports SSL-VPN, IPSEC VPN, and L2VPN.

In the next chapter, we will look at NSX security capabilities (including security composer and security groups) and learn about mapping security policies to virtual machines.

6
Data Security

In this chapter, we will look at the data security aspects of NSX. One of the primary use cases of NSX is its ability to offer a comprehensive toolset for data security. We will look at what a **Service Composer** is and how it can be used to assign security services to your applications. We will look at how to create **security groups** and policies and also how to map a security policy to a group. Next, we will look at data security and install a data security policy. We will also learn how to run a data security scan on our system. We will then learn about network extensibility and how to integrate third-party services with NSX.

In this chapter, we will cover the following topics:

- Service Composer
- Data security
- Network extensibility

Service Composer

A Service Composer provides an administrator with the ability to define a scalable and tiered security policy that is independent of the underlying infrastructure or the routed topology. This feature of the NSX platform allows security to scale and also allows the security policies that are enforced at a unit level by protecting virtual to physical or physical to virtual communications and allowing event-driven security actions.

A Service Composer consists of security groups and security policies that allow you to provision security services to your virtual machines. Service Composer, in effect, has mappings between security groups, policies, and virtual machines.

Security groups are a collection of instances that you want to protect. You can group your virtual machines to be a part of a security group or can have **vCenter objects** to be a part of a security group. You can even have a security group that consists of other security groups. Also, you can define a security group to have instances that have **security tags**.

Security policies are collections of security services and their service configurations. Firewall rules, endpoint services, and network introspection services are all part of the services in a security policy. You map security policies to security groups. When a security policy is mapped to a security group, the policy applies to all the virtual machines that are part of that security group.

Security groups

We will now look at the creation of a security group in the Service Composer:

1. Go to **Home | Networking & Security | Service Composer**:

2. Click on **Security Groups** and click the + icon to add a new security group:

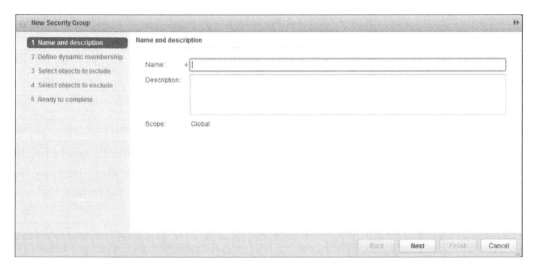

3. Enter the name of the security group. It's a good idea to have the name of the group similar to the function of the security group. For example, if the group contains instances that belong to your application, then name the group as SG-APP. Click **Next.**

4. Define the criteria that any instance or an object should meet so that it can be added to the security group. Remember that this is a dynamic action, so any object that satisfies the criteria will be part of the group:

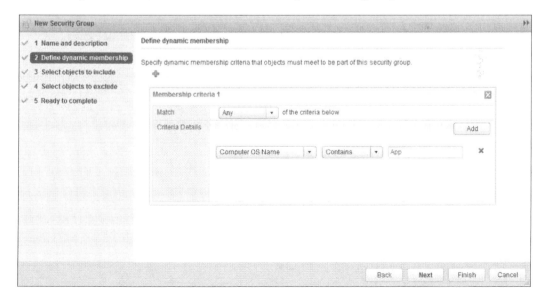

5. Clicking the **+** sign allows you to add more criteria. Within the criteria, you can click the **Add** button to add more. For example, you may want to have the security group applied to all the virtual machines whose names contain **Web**. Click on **Next** when done.

6. Select the type of objects that you want to always include in the group. This includes a range of objects including virtual machines and even other security groups. The selected objects will always be a part of the group. Click on **Next**:

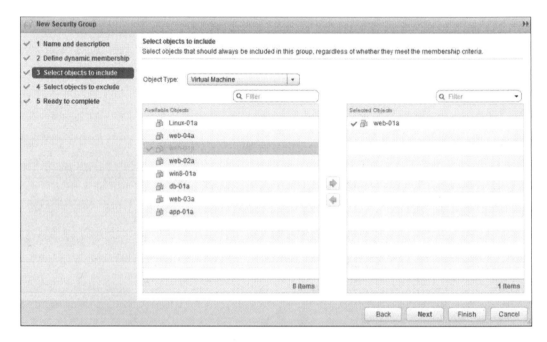

7. Select the objects that you want to exclude from the group. For example, you may want to exclude a specific virtual machine that does not need to have a security group applied to it such as a DMZ web server. Click **Next**:

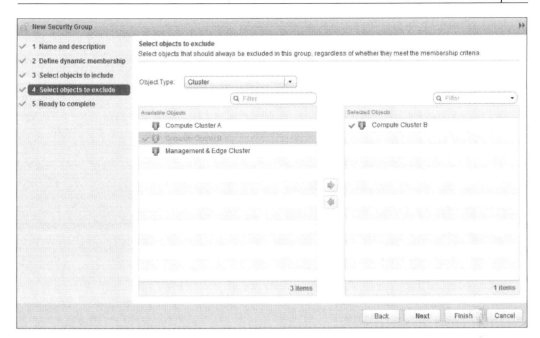

8. Review the summary and click **Finish** to create the security group:

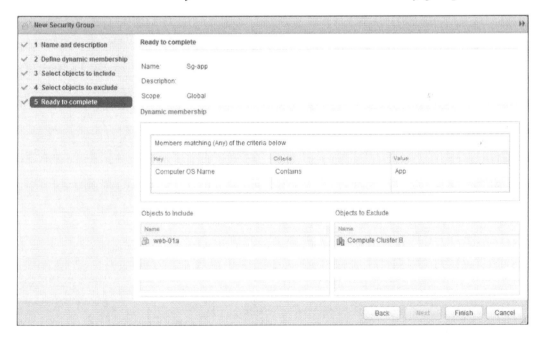

You have now successfully created a security group:

We now will create a security policy and associate it with this security group.

Security policies

Security policies are the set of rules that apply to a virtual machine, network, or firewall service. Security policies are **reusable rulesets** that can be applied to security groups. Security policies express three types of rulesets, as follows:

- Endpoint services: These are guest-based services such as anti-virus solutions and vulnerability management
- Firewall rules: These are distributed firewall policies
- Network introspection services: These are network services such as an intrusion detection system and encryption

These rules are applied to all the objects and virtual machines that are a part of a security group to which a particular policy is associated. The order of the policies applied depends on their assigned weight. The weight of a policy determines the order in which the list of the policy rules will apply.

You need to ensure that you have some introspection services installed and configured such as the distributed firewall. We looked at how to enable a distributed firewall in *Chapter 3, NSX Installation and Configuration*:

1. Go to **Home | Networking & Security | Service Composer**:

2. Click on **Security Policies**. Click on the + icon on the left-hand side to add a new security policy:

3. Click on the **+** icon on the left-hand side to add a new security policy:

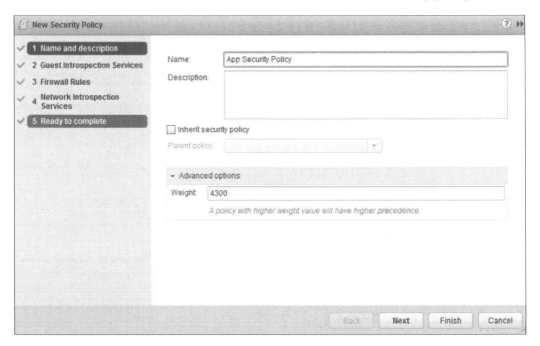

4. Enter **Name** and **Description** for the policy. Select **Inherit security policy** to allow the policy to inherit rules from another policy. This allows you to better manage policies and reduce unnecessary duplication of rules.

5. Under the advanced options, set the weight accordingly. A policy with the highest value of **Weight** is given the first precedence. By default, a new policy has the highest weight. Click on **Next** when done.

6. Under **Guest introspection services**, click the **+** icon to add a new guest introspection service:

7. Enter **Name** and **Description** for the service. Enter the default action for the service. The actions are as follows:

   ○ If you choose the **Apply** action, ensure that the VMware data security is configured and in place.

   ○ If you choose the **Block** action, select the service type:

8. Select **Service Name** as applicable for guest introspection. You will see more service names offered by a third-party vendor who integrates these services with NSX. We will look at the integration of third-party services later in the chapter.

9. Select **State** to enable or disable a defined service.

10. Select the value for **Enforce**. Enforcing allows you to prevent any changes to this policy. If another policy inherits from this policy, then enforce forces this policy to be applied before the new policy is applied.

11. Click on **OK** and then **Next** when done. You may also export the services by clicking the 1 items ⬇ ▾ icon.

Now, let's add a new firewall rule by performing the following steps:

1. Click on the **+** icon to create a new firewall rule:

2. Enter **Name** and **Description** for the rule and set an appropriate action.

3. Click on **Change** to select the source for which this policy applies. You can specify a specific security group to which this policy applies.

4. Click on **Change** to select the destination security group for this policy.

5. Clicking on **Negate destination** allows the source to access all the security groups except the one you have selected.

6. Click **Change** to select the services or service groups this rule will apply to. You can also create custom services, if needed.

7. Select the state for this rule and the log setting and click on **OK**. The rules defined here show up in the firewall table.

> Note: VMware recommends that you do not edit the Service Composer rules that are listed in the firewall table, as the rules are managed by the Service Composer. Doing so will require you to resynchronize the Service Composer rules with the firewall rules by selecting the **Synchronize firewall rules** option from the **Action** menu in the **security policies tab**.

8. Click on **Ok** when done and then click on **Next**.

9. Click the **+** symbol to add a network introspection service, and the following window appears. To define the network introspection service, you need to have specific service providers (vendor appliances) integrated to your environment. We will look at a third-party integration in the upcoming sections:

10. Enter a **Name** and **Description** for the policy. Select the action to redirect to the third-party service.

11. Select the service name and the profile of the network introspection service provider or vendor.

12. Click on **Change** to select the source and destination security groups for the policy.

13. Click on **Change** to select a specific service that you want to add.

14. Select the **State** and **Log options** and click **Ok**.

15. Click on **Next** when done.

16. Review the summary and click **Finish.**

17. The policy has now been created and added as seen in the following screenshot:

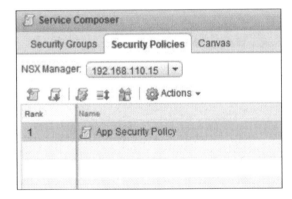

You can click on the policy to review it:

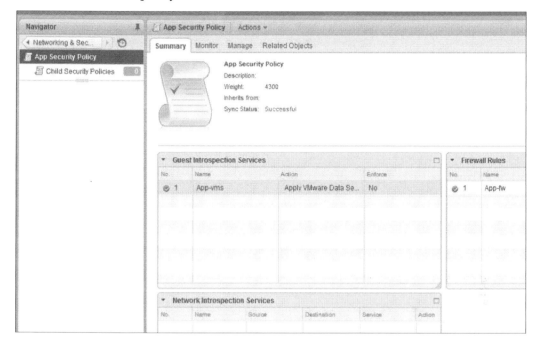

Mapping security groups and security policies

Now that we have a security group and a security policy configured, we now need to map the security policy to a security group. All the objects that are a part of the security group have the security policy rules applied to them. Objects can be dynamically added to the security group based on the criteria they meet. Perform the following steps to map the security policy to a security group:

1. Go to **Home | Networking & Security | Service Composer | Security Policies**:

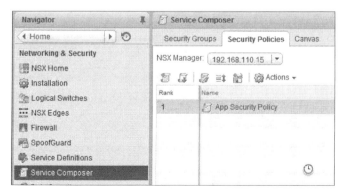

2. Select a security policy and click on the 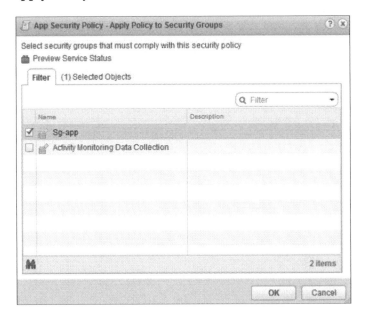 icon to associate the policy to a security group. Alternatively, you may also right-click on the policy and select **Apply Policy**:

3. Select the security group you want this policy to be associated with. You can also click on **Preview Service Status** to identify any service that will not be applied to the group:

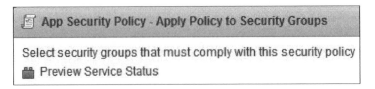

4. Click on **Preview Service Status**.

5. For example, the following snapshot shows that the VMware Data Security is not installed on the host:

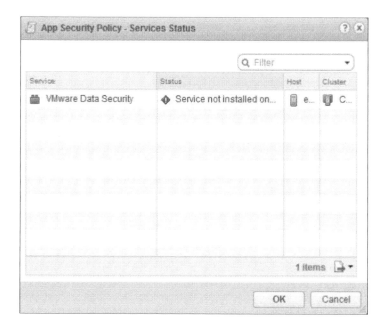

6. Click **Ok** when done. We now have a security policy associated with a security group.

There are actions that can be performed on a security policy:

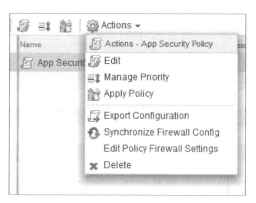

The **Manage Priority** option lets you to manage the order of the policy by placing it over or under any other rules. The **Export Configuration** option lets you export the policy configuration. **Apply Policy** maps the policy to a security group.

The **Synchronize Firewall Config** option allows you to synchronize the firewall configuration. Firewall rules in the security policy show up in the firewall configuration section. VMware does not recommend you to edit the composer rules in the firewall section. Always edit rules in the security policy and click **Synchronize Firewall Config** to apply changes appropriately.

Go to **Home | Networking & Security | Firewall**. You will see your composer rules with the associated group listed as follows:

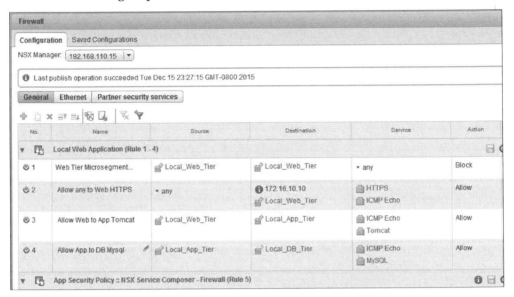

Data security

NSX data security gives you the ability to perform a scan inside your environment to report violations of predefined policies that ensure data security for sensitive data. You create a policy, and data security can scan your vSphere inventory to report violations. The installation of NSX data security involves a data security service enabled on the guest introspection service appliance. NSX supports PCI-, PHI-, and PII-related regulations only.

Before we begin installing data security, the **guest introspection service** needs to be deployed. This installs a new VIB and a service virtual machine on each host in the cluster. Guest introspection is required for NSX data security, activity monitoring, and several third-party security solutions.

 Please note: NSX supports PCI-, PHI-, and PII-related regulations only.

To deploy the guest introspection service, do the following steps:

1. Go to **Home** | **Network & Security** | **Installation** | **Service Deployments**:

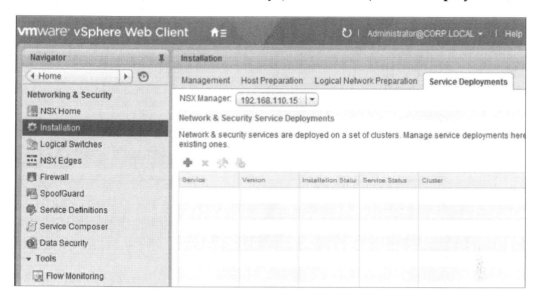

2. Click the **+** icon:

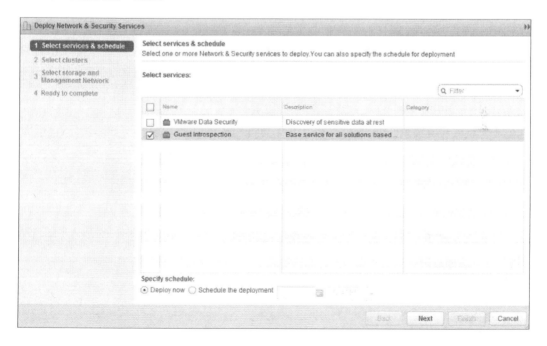

3. Select **Guest Introspection** and click on **Next.**

4. Select one more cluster where the service needs to be deployed. This has to be the same cluster where you intend to deploy the NSX data security to run scans. Click **Next:**

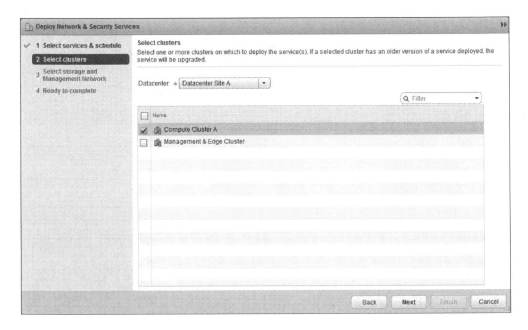

5. Select the location where the appliance will be deployed and click **Next:**

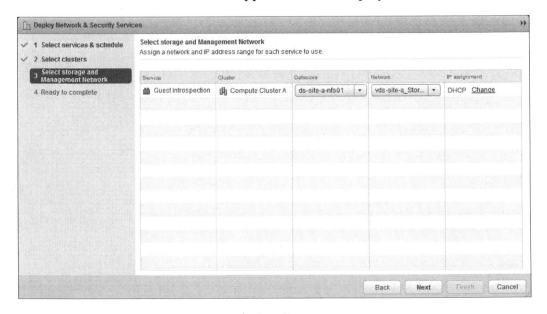

6. Review the summary and click on **Finish** to deploy. This deploys the guest introspection appliance:

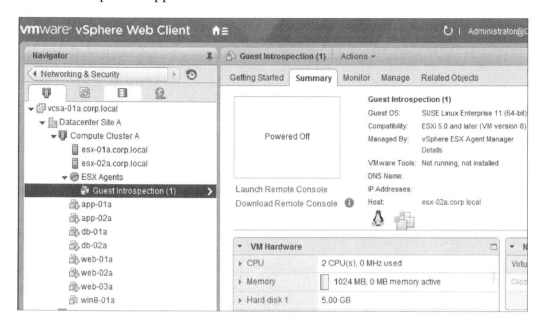

Now that we have the guest introspection service installed, we can now proceed to deploy the NSX data security service:

1. Go to **Home | Network & Security | Installation | Service Deployments**:

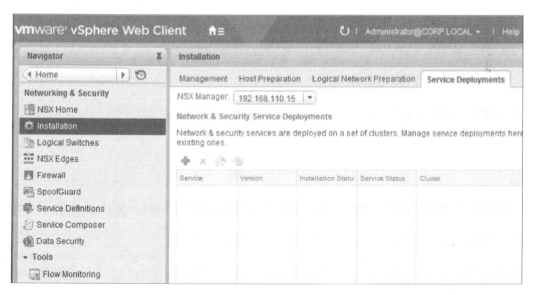

2. Click the + icon:

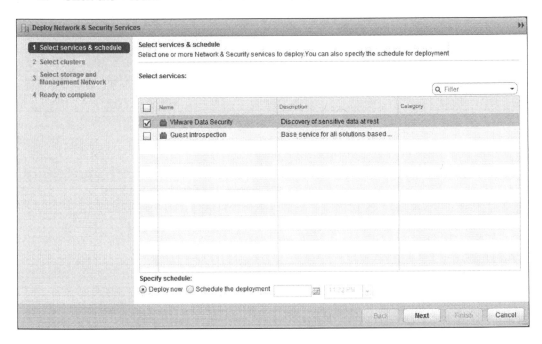

3. Select **VMware Data Security** and click on **Next**.

4. Select the cluster in which you intend to scan the environment. This cluster should also be configured for guest introspection services. Click **Next**:

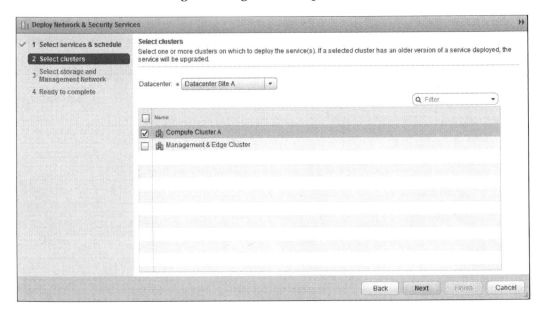

5. Select the location where the appliance will be deployed. Notice the IP assignment that also allows you to enter a static IP, if necessary. Click **Next**:

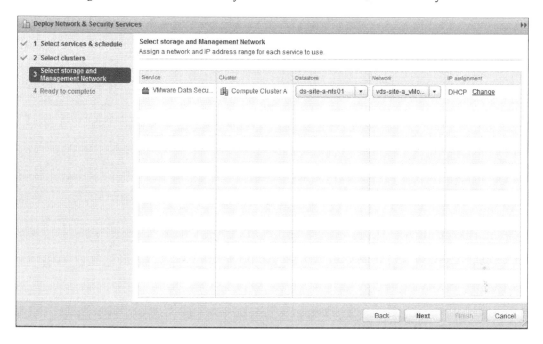

6. Review the summary and click **Finish**.

7. You will see the NSX data security appliance service being configured and enabled:

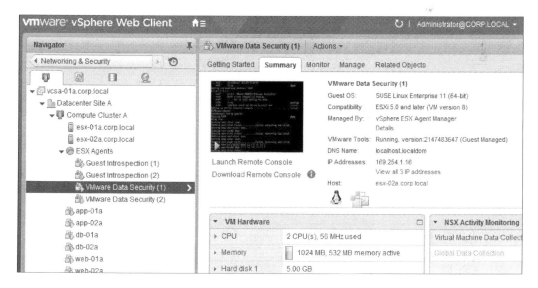

Note: The guest introspection services appliance requires minimal resources that include 2 CPUs, 1GB RAM, and 5GB of disk space. There is also one appliance deployed per host in a cluster as shown in the preceding figure.

Now that we have the NSX Data Security service installed, we will create a data security policy that allows us to detect sensitive data in our environment. A policy is defined by specifying the file filters that allow you to exclude specific data from being scanned and regulations that define specific laws such as **PCI (Payment Card Industry)** or **PHI (Protected Health Information)**.

To select regulations that apply to your organization, follow these steps:

1. Go to **Home | Networking & Security | Data Security | Manage:**

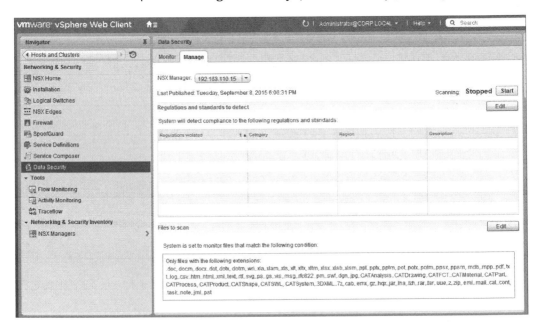

2. After clicking on **Edit**, the following window opens:

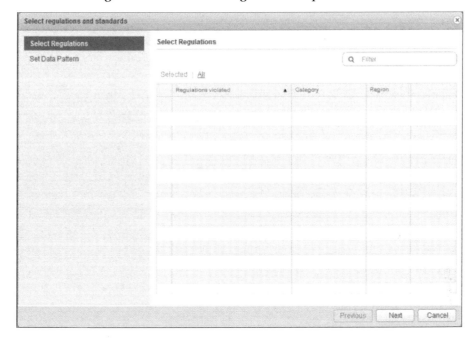

3. In the previous screenshot, clicking on **All** displays all the available regulations. Select the regulation that applies to your instances and click **Next**:

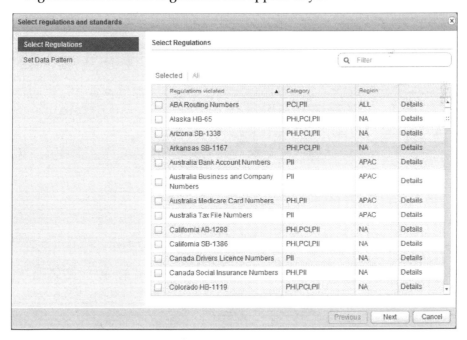

4. Certain regulations may require pattern-matching regular expressions to be able to identify data. For example, selecting the **Patient Identification Numbers** regulation requires a regex that allows you to identify proper numbers during a scan.

5. Click finish and click **Publish changes** when done.

Now that we have defined specific regulations that apply to our organization, let's create a filter to identify files that do not need to be monitored.

1. Continuing from the preceding steps, under **Files to scan**, you will find the following screenshot. Then, click on **Edit**:

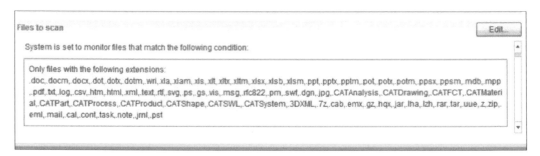

2. After clicking on **Edit**, the **Specify files to monitor** window opens:

3. Selecting **Monitor all files on the guest Virtual Machines** enables the NSX data security scan of all the files on all virtual machines.

4. Selecting **Monitor only files that match the following conditions** allows you to identify files using their size, last modified date, and type.

5. Click **Save** and **Publish Changes** when done.

Now that we have the NSX data security setup, let's look at how to run a scan:

1. Go to **Home| Networking & Security | Data Security | Manage:**

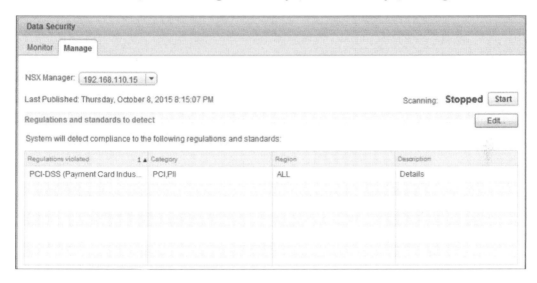

2. Click **Start** to start the scanning of the virtual machines. Only those virtual machines that are powered on are scanned.

3. Once the scan is complete, go to the **Monitor** tab to download the reports:

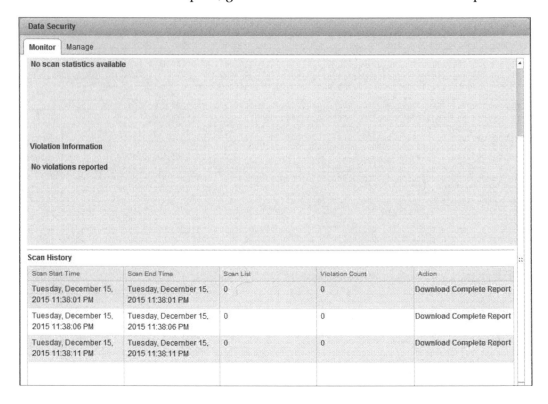

Network extensibility

We will briefly look at network extensibility, as it is a vast and fairly complex topic that covers multiple vendors and deployment architectures. NSX has the ability to integrate with multiple vendors to provide a rich network feature set and also a single pane of glass to manage multiple physical network devices.

A third-party service provider (vendor) must register with the NSX manager using the specified login credentials. Once registered, we will deploy the partner service that allows NSX to offer a third-party service:

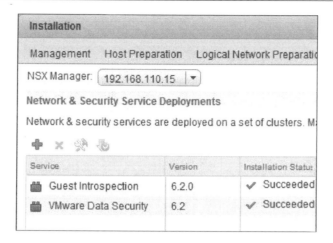

Earlier while creating security policies, we saw the option that allows traffic to be redirected to the third-party services. You may also redirect traffic by adding firewall rules. Click on the **Partner security services** tab in the **Firewall** section:

During the creation of the new rule, select **Action** as **Redirect** to allow traffic redirection to a third-party vendor.

Summary

One of the most important factors for a successful enterprise is compliance and security. We started this chapter by looking at Service Composer. We created service groups with a dynamic grouping of virtual machines and vCenter objects. We also created a service policy and associated that with a service group. We installed the NSX data security service and selected the applicable regulations from the list provided. These regulations are specific to my organization's needs. We also investigated the file filter to exclude any file types that do not need to be scanned. We also ran a data security scan. NSX can integrate with partner services, and we looked at a very generic integration process. We briefly discussed security policies and firewall rule redirection as well.

In the next chapter, we will look at the monitoring of our environment using the tools offered by NSX. We will look at activity monitoring, flow monitoring, and Traceflow, among others.

7
Monitoring

In this chapter, we will be looking at the monitoring of our environment and the different tools NSX has to offer. We will begin the chapter by looking at **Activity Monitoring** that allows us to have a visibility of applications to verify that security policies are being enforced appropriately. We will also look at how to enable **data collection** on one or more virtual machines. We will also view a virtual machine activity report. We will then discuss **flow monitoring** and the **Traceflow** feature.

In this chapter, we will cover the following topics:

- Activity Monitoring
- Virtual machine activity reports
- Flow monitoring
- Traceflow

Activity Monitoring

Activity Monitoring provides insight and visibility into applications running within an operating system to ensure that the security policies are being enforced correctly. For example, Activity Monitoring can help if you have a misconfigured web server that receives traffic on HTTP instead of HTTPS as it's supposed to. Activity monitoring lets you run reports to monitor inbound and outbound traffic to the machines managed by the vCenter.

 Activity Monitoring is supported only on Windows virtual machines. Linux virtual machines are not supported as of the NSX 6.2 version.

The prerequisites for Activity Monitoring require a guest introspection to be installed. On the virtual machines, you will need to install a guest introspection driver that is a part of the VMware tools installation. A full installation typically installs the driver onto the operating system. The purpose of the guest introspection driver (VMCI Driver) is to detect all the applications running on the operating system and to send this information to the guest introspection appliance.

You are also required to have NSX Manager configured with your active directory so that it can have access to different user groups. We will look at how to configure NSX with an active directory in *Chapter 8, Managing NSX*. We will then install the guest introspection appliance virtual machine. The installation for the guest introspection virtual machines has been described in *Chapter 6, Data Security*.

To enable the Activity Monitoring feature on the Windows virtual machine, do the following:

1. Select the desired Windows virtual machine and click on the **Summary** tab.

2. Click on **Edit** under **NSX Activity Monitoring** to enable the virtual machine data collection:

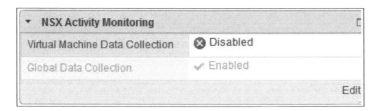

3. You will be presented with a prompt, as follows:

4. Click on **Yes** and the following **NSX Activity Monitoring** window opens:

5. Alternatively, you can use the service composer to define a dynamic membership for the virtual machines. This can be associated to an **Activity Monitoring Data Collection** service group to allow dynamic membership of virtual machines for data collection.

 Activity Monitoring Data Collection is a predefined service group.

Virtual machine activity report

Now that we have data collection enabled, we will be able to create an activity report for our Windows virtual machine:

1. Go to **Networking & Security | Activity Monitoring**:

2. Click on the **VM Activity** tab.

3. Click on the link beside **Where source VM** that allows you to select the virtual machine for which the outbound traffic needs to be monitored.

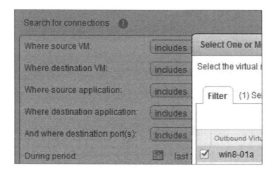

4. Click on the link beside **Where destination VM** that allows you to select the virtual machine to which the inbound traffic needs to be monitored.

5. You can select the time period by clicking the **During period** option.

6. Click on **Search**.

7. You may also export the search results in the `.csv` format by clicking the icon in the lower-right corner.

Flow Monitoring

NSX Flow Monitoring is a feature that allows detailed traffic monitoring to and from protected virtual machines. Flow Monitoring can uniquely identify different machines and different services that exchange data, and when enabled, it can identify which machines are exchanging data over specific applications. Flow Monitoring also allows the live monitoring of TCP and UDP connections and can be used as an effective forensic tool.

 Flow Monitoring can only be turned on for NSX deployments where the firewall is enabled.

The Flow Monitoring data can be polled to a set interval and then analyzed. The default period is 24 hours and the minimum is 1 hour, while the maximum data collection interval is 2 weeks. Keep an eye on the disk space being consumed by NSX Manager as the polling interval is set.

To view the Flow Monitoring data, follow these steps:

1. Log in to your vCenter web client and navigate to **Networking & Security |
   Flow Monitoring**:

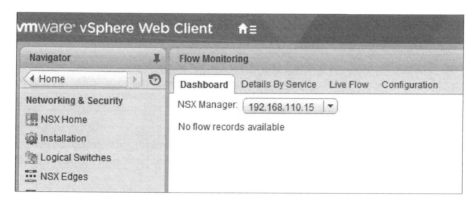

2. Click on **Flow Monitoring** under the **Dashboard** tab:

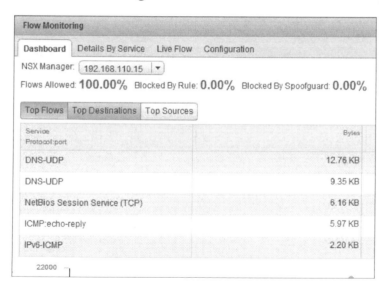

3. To change the time interval, click on the 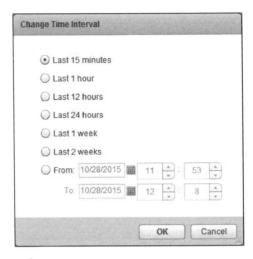 icon on the right-hand side to change the time interval for the flow:

4. You will see the flows that are allowed, blocked by rule, and blocked by spoofguard metrics:

5. The **Top Flows** tab shows the overall incoming and outgoing traffic over the specified period of time:

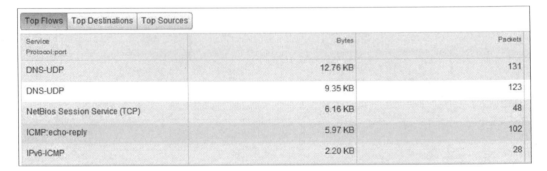

Top Flows	Top Destinations	Top Sources		
Service Protocol:port			Bytes	Packets
DNS-UDP			12.76 KB	131
DNS-UDP			9.35 KB	123
NetBios Session Service (TCP)			6.16 KB	48
ICMP:echo-reply			5.97 KB	102
IPv6-ICMP			2.20 KB	28

6. The **Top Destinations** tab shows the incoming traffic per destination, while the **Top Sources** tab shows the specified outgoing traffic per source:

Top Flows	Top Destinations	Top Sources		
Destination		Incoming Traffic (Bytes)		Packets
192.168.110.10		15.51 KB		171
fd53::11		12.97 KB		134
8.8.8.8		5.74 KB		98
win8-01a (fe80::d1fc:198e:f37e:aa37)		904		11
00:50:56:01:20:a5		598		13

7. The **Top Sources** tab shows the outgoing traffic per source as follows:

Top Flows	Top Destinations	Top Sources		
Source		Outgoing Traffic (Bytes)		Packets
win8-01a (192.168.100.222)		21.64 KB		275
win8-01a (fe80::d1fc:198e:f37e:aa37)		13.74 KB		145
fe80::1		744		7
00:50:56:01:20:a5		598		13
00:50:56:ae:09:87		598		13

8. The **Details By Service** tab shows the allowed and blocked flows including the number of sessions per type of flow. You can click on the service to view the traffic flow and the rules that apply. You can also choose to edit a rule by clicking on **Edit Rule** in the **Actions** column, or you can add a rule by clicking on **Add Rule** in the **Actions** column.

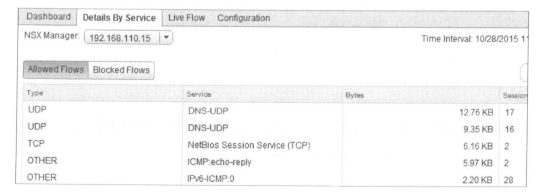

Dashboard	Details By Service	Live Flow	Configuration	
NSX Manager: 192.168.110.15 ▼				Time Interval: 10/28/2015 1

Allowed Flows   Blocked Flows

Type	Service	Bytes	Session
UDP	DNS-UDP	12.76 KB	17
UDP	DNS-UDP	9.35 KB	16
TCP	NetBios Session Service (TCP)	6.16 KB	2
OTHER	ICMP:echo-reply	5.97 KB	2
OTHER	IPv6-ICMP:0	2.20 KB	28

One of the most interesting features is the ability to see a live flow for a selected vNIC. You can monitor all the live TCP and UDP connections to a vNIC using the **live flow feature**. To do so, perform the following set of steps:

 You can monitor a maximum of two vNICs per host and a maximum of five vNICs per vCenter.

1. Log in to vCenter web client and go to **Networking & Security | Flow Monitoring**.

2. Click on **Live Flow** in the dashboard:

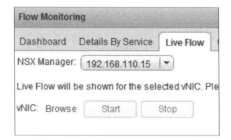

3. Click on **Browse** to select a vNIC and then click on **Start** when done.

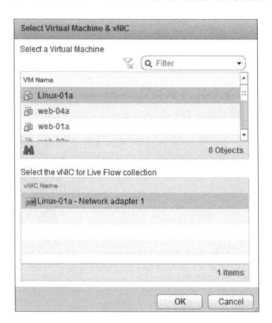

The refresh rate can be set accordingly.

4. Click on **Stop** when done.

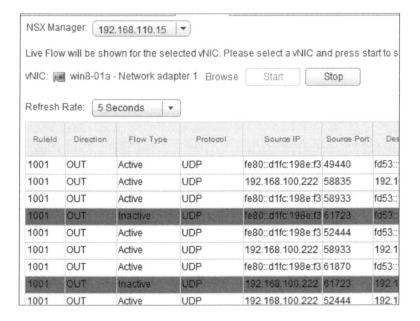

 Using live flow increases NSX Manager's resource consumption, so this feature should be used sparingly.

Traceflow

Traceflow is an interesting tool and was built with the purpose of allowing an administrator to seamlessly troubleshoot their virtual network environment by tracing a packet flow similar to the legacy Packet Tracer application. Traceflow allows you to **inject** a packet into the network and monitor its flow across the network. This flow allows you to monitor your network and identify issues such as bottlenecks or disruptions.

Traceflow allows you to construct your own packets with custom headers and packet sizes. The target destination of this test packet can be a NSX-managed overlay network or underlay network devices such as a host or a logical router. The source will always be a vNIC from a VM. These packets are injected in the virtual distributed switch and support Layer 2 unicast, multicast, and broadcast and layer 3 unicast traffic types.

To use Traceflow, follow these steps:

1. Log in to your vCenter web client and go to **Networking & Security |
   Traceflow**:

2. Select the appropriate traffic type. You can pick among **Unicast, L2
   Multicast**, and **L2 Broadcast**.

3. Select the vNIC of the source VM from where the packet will be sent.

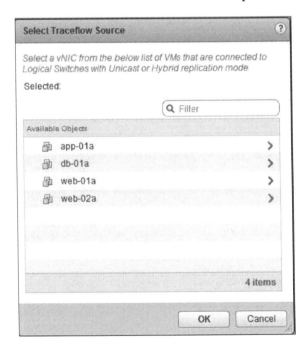

4. You can click on the right arrow to select the vNIC.

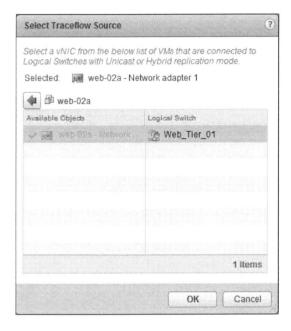

5. Select **Traceflow Destination** and you will get the following window:

6. If **L2 Broadcast** traceflow is selected, enter the value for **Subnet Prefix Length**:

Trace Parameters

Traffic Type: [L2 Broadcast ▼] ⚠ High volume of traffic may get generated for this traffic type.

Source: ✳ 🖥 web-02a - Network adapter 1 Change...   Subnet Prefix Length: ✳ [   ]
         IP: 172.16.10.12, MAC: 00:50:56:ae:19:72

▸ Advanced Options

7. For layer 2 multicast traceflow, multicast group addresses are entered:

Trace Parameters

Traffic Type: [L2 Multicast ▼] ⚠ High volume of traffic may get generated for this traffic type.

Source: ✳ 🖥 web-02a - Network adapter 1 Change...   Destination IP: ✳ [   ]   e.g. 239.0.0.1
         IP: 172.16.10.12, MAC: 00:50:56:ae:19:72

8. You may leave the advanced options as default unless your network tests require a certain scenario to be created:

▾ Advanced Options

Protocol:	[ICMP ▼]	Timeout (ms):	[10000]
ICMP ID:	[0]	Frame Size:	[128]
Sequence:	[0]	TTL:	[64]

9. Click **Trace** when done.

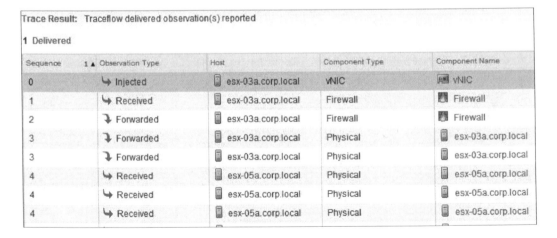

Trace Result: Traceflow delivered observation(s) reported

1 Delivered

Sequence 1 ▲	Observation Type	Host	Component Type	Component Name
0	↳ Injected	🖥 esx-03a.corp.local	vNIC	🖥 vNIC
1	↳ Received	🖥 esx-03a.corp.local	Firewall	🖥 Firewall
2	↴ Forwarded	🖥 esx-03a.corp.local	Firewall	🖥 Firewall
3	↴ Forwarded	🖥 esx-03a.corp.local	Physical	🖥 esx-03a.corp.local
3	↴ Forwarded	🖥 esx-03a.corp.local	Physical	🖥 esx-03a.corp.local
4	↳ Received	🖥 esx-05a.corp.local	Physical	🖥 esx-05a.corp.local
4	↳ Received	🖥 esx-05a.corp.local	Physical	🖥 esx-05a.corp.local
4	↳ Received	🖥 esx-05a.corp.local	Physical	🖥 esx-05a.corp.local

In the following image, you can see that the packet was successfully delivered and the entire trace is visible.

4	⤷ Received	📱 esx-01a.corp.local	Physical	📱 esx-01a.corp.local
4	⤷ Received	📱 esx-01a.corp.local	Physical	📱 esx-01a.corp.local
5	⤷ Received	📱 esx-01a.corp.local	Firewall	🔳 Firewall
6	⤴ Forwarded	📱 esx-01a.corp.local	Firewall	🔳 Firewall
7	✔ Delivered	📱 esx-01a.corp.local	vNIC	🔲 vNIC

Summary

We started this chapter with by looking at three interesting tools that NSX offers to allow us to efficiently and thoroughly monitor and analyze our environment. Activity Monitoring is a tool that gives us a visibility of applications. Remember to have VMware data security and guest introspection services deployed before using these tools. Also, Activity Monitoring is supported only on Windows virtual machines. You will also need to enable guest introspection in the VMware tools. We then looked at the virtual machine activity report followed by Flow Monitoring. We ended the chapter by looking at the traceflow tool to identify network issues. This tool allows us to have end-to-end packet trace visibility.

In the next chapter, we will look at the operational management of our NSX environment. We will look at how to back up NSX Manager and set up syslog servers, controller cluster actions, and many more.

8
Managing NSX

In this chapter, we will be looking at some of the most common operations for managing our NSX environment. We will begin the chapter by looking at NSX Manager actions that include **backing up and restoring** your NSX environment and management settings including the setting up of **syslog servers** and NSX with a Windows domain. We will also look at controller cluster actions that include changing passwords, taking a controller snapshot, and recovering from controller failure. We will also look at how to check communication channel health for communications between NSX Manager and its associated components.

In this chapter, we will cover the following topics:

- NSX Manager settings
- Backup and restore
- NSX Manager domain registration
- Controller cluster actions

NSX Manager settings

There are several settings in NSX Manager that can be edited to suit your environment. These settings can also be edited using the NSX CLI; however, we will look at how to update these settings using the UI.

Date and time

You can change the date and time settings as needed.

 An NSX Manager reboot is needed after a date or time change is made.

You need to perform the following steps:

1. Log in to the NSX Manager virtual machine appliance.

2. Click on **Appliance Management** and then on **Manage Appliance**, and the following window appears:

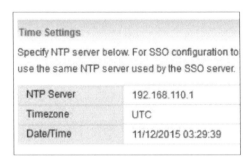

3. Next to **Time Settings**, click on the **Edit** tab:

4. Click on **OK** when done.

5. Reboot the appliance to apply the changes.

Syslog server

It is recommended to have a syslog server. Configuring NSX Manager with a remote syslog server enables you to collect, view, and save all log files to a central location. This enables you to store logs for compliance purposes and, when using a tool such as **VMware's vRealize log insght**, it enables you to create alarms and use the built-in search engine to review logs.

The steps to configure NSX Manager to start forwarding logs to a syslog server are as follows:

1. Log in to the NSX Manager virtual appliance.

2. Click on **Manage Appliance Settings** and then click on **General**.

3. Locate **Syslog Server** and click on **Edit** next to it and the following window appears:

4. Enter the syslog server values as applicable and click on **OK**:

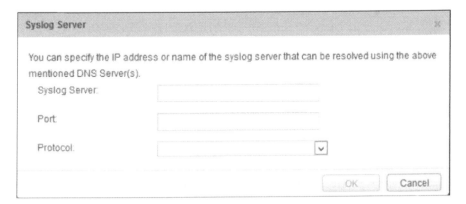

DNS servers

It is important to have DNS configured in your environment and to have NSX
Manager configured to be used as a DNS server. The steps to configure NSX
Manager to be used as a DNS server are as follows:

1. Log in to the NSX Manager virtual appliance.

2. Click on **Manage Appliance Settings** and go to **Network**.

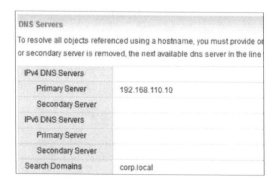

3. Locate **DNS Servers** and click on **Edit** next to it. The following window
    appears:

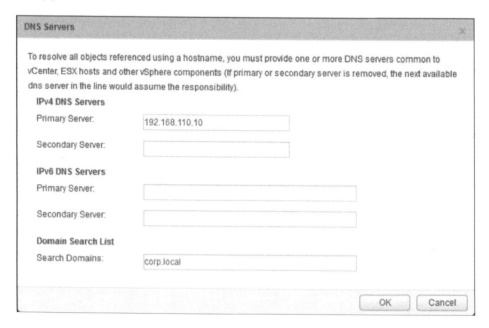

4. Enter the DNS server values and click on **OK** when done.

Technical support logs

During NSX troubleshooting, you will be required to download the technical support logs in order to review them and submit them to VMware technical support. The steps are as follows:

1. Log in to the NSX Manager virtual appliance.

2. Click on **Manage Appliance Settings**.

3. In the right-hand corner of the screen, click on the ⚙ icon and then click on **Download Tech Support Log**:

4. Click on **Download**. NSX Manager will now prepare the log bundle, and when it is ready, click on **Save** to download the log bundle to your desktop. The log bundle is compressed and downloaded as a .gz file.

SSL certificates

NSX Manager generates a self-signed certificate during the initial installation; however, you can also configure it to use a CA-signed certificate to authenticate its identity and secure communication. VMware recommends that you generate the certificate using NSX Manager's **Generate Certificate** option. The process of registering a certificate includes generating a certificate, signing it with a CA, and then importing the signed certificate.

To generate a **Certificate Signing Request (CSR)**, follow these steps:

1. Log in to the NSX Manager virtual appliance.

2. Click on **Manage Appliance Settings** and navigate to **SSL Certificates**:

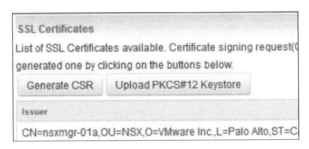

3. Click on **Generate CSR** to generate the SSL certificate as follows:

4. Complete the form appropriately and click on **OK** when done.

Now that the CSR has been generated, download the certificate by clicking on **Download CSR**. You will now send this to your CA to get it signed. Use the **Import** option to upload the signed certificates that you receive from the CA. Save your signed certificates.

Backup and restore

Backups are critical for the NSX environment that allows you to restore them appropriately during a system failure. Apart from vCenter, you can also perform backup operations of NSX Manager, controller clusters, NSX Edge, firewall rules, and service composer. All these can be backed up and restored individually.

NSX Manager backup

NSX Manager can be backed up on-demand or on a schedule basis. NSX Manager backups are saved over the FTP or SFTP that NSX Manager can access.

 NSX Manager restore is supported for the same NSX Manager version as the backup.

Perform the following set of steps to back up and restore data:

1. Log in to NSX Manager via the web access.
2. Click on **Backups & Restore**.

3. Next to FTP server settings, click on **Change** to specify the backup location:

4. Fill in the appropriate fields and click on **OK**.

5. Clicking on **Backup** takes an on-demand backup:

6. To schedule a backup, click on **Change** near the **Schedule** option to set a schedule:

In the event of a failure that requires a restore operation, redeploy a fresh NSX Manager of the same backup version, configure the FTP server settings, and use the **Restore** option to restore a backup.

It is recommended that a **controller snapshot** be taken at the same time as NSX Manager. Doing so allows the backup data to be **synchronized** across NSX Manager and the controller. To take a controller snapshot, follow these steps:

1. Log in to the vSphere web client and navigate to **Home | Network & Security | Installation | Management**.

2. Under the NSX controller nodes, select a node and click the  (Download Controller Snapshot) icon.

3. Click the **Download** button to download the snapshot:

A restore of the controller snapshots should only be done by the VMware technical support only.

As part of NSX Manager backup, the NSX edge appliance configuration is also backed up. The edge appliances include logical routers and also edge services gateway appliances. Inaccessible or failed NSX edge appliances can be redeployed using the **Redeploy NSX Edge** action.

A firewall configuration can be exported using the **Export** icon in the firewall section. This exports all the firewall configuration and rules in the XML format that can be downloaded and saved to a safe location. This also contains NSX service composer rules.

Any service composer configuration can be backed up by exporting it. This is done using the **Export Service Configuration** option found under **Actions** in any security policy that you pick. The configuration is downloaded to a select location on your desktop, which can then be moved to a safe location. The downloaded configuration can also be imported to another NSX Manager.

NSX Manager domain registration

It is recommended to register your NSX deployment with your Windows domain. This allows NSX to map user and group information and the associations as well, which allows you to create security bindings based on these relationships.

Register a domain to your NSX Manager with the following procedure:

1. Log in to the vSphere web client, navigate to **Home** | **Networking & Security** | **NSX Managers**, select your NSX Manager, and go to **Manage** | **Domains**:

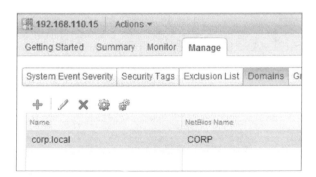

2. Click the **+** sign to add a new domain.

3. Enter a fully qualified domain name.

4. Specify the domain controller with which the domain needs to be synchronized. Select the protocol.

5. Enter the user credentials of the account and click on **Next**.

6. Select **Use Domain Credentials** if you want to authenticate using the LDAP server.

7. Click on **Next** and click on **Finish** when done.

By default, all domains are synchronized automatically every 3 hours. Under NSX Managers, go to the **Name** columns and then the **Manage** tab. Click on the appropriate synchronization technique. While **delta synchronization** synchronizes only the changed AD objects, a **full synchronization** does a complete refresh of all AD objects.

Controller cluster operations

There are certain operations that can be performed on a controller cluster. You should always change the **default password** for the controller clusters to ensure data security.

To change the passwords on a controller cluster, follow these steps:

1. Log in to the vSphere web client and go to **Home | Networking & Security | Installation**.

2. The **Management** tab shows the list of controllers. Pick the one in which a password needs to be changed. It is recommended that all three controllers have different passwords.

3. Click on **Actions** and go to **Change Controller Cluster Password**:

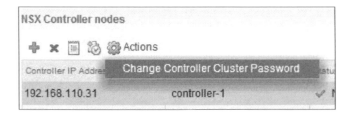

4. Enter a new password and click **OK** when done.

The control plane remains unaffected in the event that a single NSX controller fails. However, VMware recommends redeployment of the entire cluster and using the **Update Controller State** mechanism to synchronize the state of the controller cluster.

 Updating Controller State causes logical routers to be redeployed and VXLAN to be resynchronized.

The following steps are used to deploy a fresh controller cluster:

1. Log in to the vSphere web client and navigate to **Home | Networking & Security | Installation | Management**.

2. Delete the NSX Controllers by clicking on each one of them and clicking the ✖ (Delete) icon.

3. Deploy a new set of NSX controllers using the standard NSX controller deployment steps.

4. Once deployed, go to the NSX Manager pane under the **Management** tab and click on **Actions** and then, **Update Controller State**:

NSX Manager constantly checks on the health of the communication between the NSX Manager and all of its deployed components. To check on the status of the communication channel health, follow these steps:

1. Log in to vSphere web client and go to **Home | Networking & Security | Installation | Host preparation**.

2. Select a cluster and expand it. Select any host and click on **Actions** and then **Communication Channel Health**:

The communication channel health information is displayed, as follows:

Summary

We started this chapter by looking at the NSX Manager settings. We looked at many settings that included changing the date and time, configuring a syslog server, configuring DNS servers, gathering tech support logs, and configuring SSL certificates. We then looked at the backup and restore of our NSX Manager including taking a look at NSX controller snapshots. Also, we looked at how to configure our NSX Manager with an Active Directory. The section on NSX Controller operations described how to change the NSX controller passwords, which is the best practice, and also talked about how to properly recover from a failed controller state. Finally, we reviewed the communication channel health between NSX Manager and all of its components.

9
Conclusion

By now, you should have a pretty good understanding of NSX and feel comfortable using it. In this book, we went over the basics and the step-by-step deployment of NSX and its features. It is important to understand that this is not the end, but in fact the beginning of the NSX ecosystem. There is a lot more to learn and understand about NSX; however, the eight chapters with which we spent time together will give you a head start.

There are lots of other articles about NSX that are worth reading along with this book. In this concluding chapter, I will list out these recommended articles that you can go over to get a continuous understanding of NSX features and use cases:

- First, there is always VMware's NSX documentation. NSX documentation is very well written and has a lot of information that will help you further. More specifically, you should read up on the administration guide. The administration guide is given at: `http://pubs.vmware.com/NSX-62/topic/com.vmware.ICbase/PDF/nsx_62_admin.pdf`

- You can also read the NSX design guide. Although this was written for version 6.1, its concepts are still valid and gives you a pretty good idea of some of the industry's best practices and design considerations when deploying NSX components, features, and services. You can get the guide from here: `https://www.vmware.com/files/pdf/products/nsx/vmw-nsx-network-virtualization-design-guide.pdf`

- It's easy enough to deploy NSX in a greenfield environment; however, when it comes to brownfield environments, this technical white paper can be quite helpful in getting you started: `https://www.vmware.com/files/pdf/products/nsx/VMware-NSX-Brownfield-Design-and-Deployment-Guide.pdf`

- There are a lot of vendors who have provided technical white papers that are worth giving a read. Palo Alto Networks have been at the forefront of enabling its PAN firewall to work and inter-op with NSX. Here is a good technical white paper on the integration: `https://www.vmware.com/files/pdf/products/nsx/NSX-Palo-Alto-Networks-WP.pdf`

- The NSX and F5 BIG-IP design guide is another such document that would give you a lot of insight into deployment and design ideas: `https://f5.com/Portals/1/Premium/Architectures/RA-VMware-NSX-Design-Guide.pdf`

If you don't have a lab ready to go, you can always start learning NSX instantly using VMware's hands-on labs. Just go to `http://labs.hol.vmware.com/HOL/catalogs/` and explore the different NSX labs that get deployed instantly and can be accessed by any machine that has connectivity and a web browser. You will need to register to access the lab, and registration is free and open. Each lab comes with a lab exercise guide, and I recommend that you go over the labs in the following order:

- **HOL-SDC-1603 VMware NSX Introduction**: This gives you a basic hands-on introduction to NSX. Doing the exercises in order lets you deploy and test all the NSX functionalities.

- **HOL-SDC-1625 VMware NSX Advanced**: This allows you to have a deeper look into NSX, including deploying and configuring some of its advanced features.

- **HOL-SDC-1624 VMware NSX and the vRealize Suite**: vRealize Automation and other products in the vRealize suite integrate very well with NSX and can deploy network-rich services on-demand. This lab helps you to understand the integration and application of such services.

- **HOL-SDC-1620 OpenStack with VMware vSphere and NSX**: This lab gives you a closer look at integrating NSX and deploying rich services in a **VMware Integrated OpenStack (VIO)** environment.

All the preceding links will be posted on the book's website as it becomes available. Also, you can always reach me via my blog or Twitter account to discuss use cases and any issues that you may run into.

I hope you enjoyed the book and will continue on your path of consuming the rich features and services offered by NSX. I wish you all the best!

Index

Thank you for buying
Learning VMware NSX

About Packt Publishing

Packt, pronounced 'packed', published its first book, *Mastering phpMyAdmin for Effective MySQL Management*, in April 2004, and subsequently continued to specialize in publishing highly focused books on specific technologies and solutions.

Our books and publications share the experiences of your fellow IT professionals in adapting and customizing today's systems, applications, and frameworks. Our solution-based books give you the knowledge and power to customize the software and technologies you're using to get the job done. Packt books are more specific and less general than the IT books you have seen in the past. Our unique business model allows us to bring you more focused information, giving you more of what you need to know, and less of what you don't.

Packt is a modern yet unique publishing company that focuses on producing quality, cutting-edge books for communities of developers, administrators, and newbies alike. For more information, please visit our website at www.packtpub.com.

About Packt Enterprise

In 2010, Packt launched two new brands, Packt Enterprise and Packt Open Source, in order to continue its focus on specialization. This book is part of the Packt Enterprise brand, home to books published on enterprise software – software created by major vendors, including (but not limited to) IBM, Microsoft, and Oracle, often for use in other corporations. Its titles will offer information relevant to a range of users of this software, including administrators, developers, architects, and end users.

Writing for Packt

We welcome all inquiries from people who are interested in authoring. Book proposals should be sent to author@packtpub.com. If your book idea is still at an early stage and you would like to discuss it first before writing a formal book proposal, then please contact us; one of our commissioning editors will get in touch with you.

We're not just looking for published authors; if you have strong technical skills but no writing experience, our experienced editors can help you develop a writing career, or simply get some additional reward for your expertise.

[PACKT] enterprise
PUBLISHING   professional expertise distilled

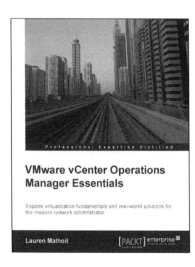

VMware vCenter Operations
Manager Essentials

Explore virtualization fundamentals and real-world solutions for
the modern network administrator

Lauren Malhoit   [PACKT] enterprise

VMware vCenter Operations Manager Essentials

ISBN: 978-1-78217-696-1   Paperback: 246 pages

Explore virtualization fundamentals and real-world solutions for the modern network administrator

1. Written by VMware expert Lauren Malhoit, this book takes a look at vCenter Operations Manager from a practical point of view that every administrator can appreciate.

2. Understand, troubleshoot, and design your virtual environment in a better and more efficient way than you ever have before.

3. A step-by-step and learn-by-example guide to understanding the ins and outs of vCenter Operations Manager.

VMware vSphere 5.x Datacenter
Design Cookbook

Over 70 recipes to design a virtual datacenter for performance,
availability, manageability, and recoverability with VMware
vSphere 5.x

Hersey Cartwright   [PACKT] enterprise

VMware vSphere 5.x Datacenter Design Cookbook

ISBN: 978-1-78217-700-5   Paperback: 260 pages

Over 70 recipes to design a virtual datacenter for performance, availability, manageability, and recoverability with VMware vSphere 5.x

1. Innovative recipes, offering numerous practical solutions when designing virtualized datacenters.

2. Identify the design factors—requirements, assumptions, constraints, and risks—by conducting stakeholder interviews and performing technical assessments.

3. Increase and guarantee performance, availability, and workload efficiency with practical steps and design considerations.

Please check **www.PacktPub.com** for information on our titles

VMware vSphere 5.1 Cookbook

ISBN: 978-1-84968-402-6   Paperback: 466 pages

Over 130 task-oriented recipes to install, configure, and manage various vSphere 5.1 components

1. Install and configure vSphere 5.1 core components.

2. Learn important aspects of vSphere such as administration, security, and performance.

3. Configure vSphere Management Assistant (VMA) to run commands/scripts without the need to authenticate every attempt.

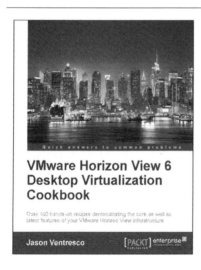

VMware Horizon View 6 Desktop Virtualization Cookbook

ISBN: 978-1-78217-164-5   Paperback: 332 pages

Over 100 hands-on recipes demonstrating the core as well as latest features of your VMware Horizon View infrastructure

1. Gain a detailed insight into the configuration and administration of core features of VMware Horizon View.

2. Learn how to deploy the newest features of the VMware Horizon View 6.0 such as Cloud Pod Architecture, VSAN integration, and more.

3. Benefit from practical examples that provide a greater level of detail than the VMware Horizon View documentation.

Please check **www.PacktPub.com** for information on our titles

VAPP for NSX controller w/ 3 VM's.

Recording Mod 4 L1-A
              L1-B
              L2-

unicast-specific
multicast - WEBEX, training sessions

Made in the USA
Lexington, KY
26 February 2016